Labradoodles

The Owners Guide from Puppy to Old
Age for Your American, British or
Australian Labradoodle Dog

By Alan Kenworthy

Copyright and Trademarks

Disclaimer and Legal Notice

Foreword

Once you've read this book you will have all the information you need in order to make a well-informed decision about whether or not the Labradoodle is the breed for you, and you will know how to care for them at every stage of their life.

As an owner, expert trainer and professional dog whisperer, I would like to teach you the human side of the equation, so you can learn how to think more like your dog and eliminate behavioral problems with your pet.

Too many backyard breeders and puppy mills produce Labradoodles and other Poodle crosses. These "breeders" have no understanding of genetics. In most cases, they don't even give bloodlines a thought. My goal here is to help you understand the positives and negatives of this emerging breed.

Adoptions through kennels working to promote the breed help to refine the quality of all Labradoodles.

I am a huge fan of Labradoodles, but I'm not going to suggest they are without their drawbacks. Also, there is NO guarantee that a Labradoodle is hypoallergenic. Many are not, and those are often the dogs surrendered to shelters.

Before you adopt a Labradoodle or any crossbred dog, these are the issues you must investigate and understand. There are no certainties with hybrids like the Labradoodle, but there are great possibilities!

More and more responsible breeders are producing excellent Labradoodles. This is not a "fad" breed, but a truly exceptional companion and one to which I look forward to introducing you.

Acknowledgments

In writing this book, I also sought tips, advice, photos and opinions from many experts of the Labradoodle breed.

In particular, I wish to thank the following wonderful experts for going out of their way to help and contribute:

USA & CANADA

Nicki Dana of Premiere Labradoodles
http://premierelabradoodles.com

Dana Eckert of California Labradoodles
http://www.californialabradoodles.us/

Rochelle Woods of Spring Creek Labradoodles
http://www.springcreeklabradoodles.com

Tracy A. Wynn of Desert Winds Labradoodles
http://www.dwdoodles.com

Becky & Jim Roth of Southern Cross Australian Labradoodles
http://www.southerncrosslabradoodles.com

Barbara Dearaujo of Dreamydoodles Northwest
http://www.dreamydoodles.com/

Karen Elliott of Rocky Mountain Labradoodles
http://www.rockymountainlabradoodles.com

Elizabeth Ferris of Country Labradoodles
http://www.australian-labradoodle.com

Acknowledgments

Jessica & Nelson Guthrie of Labradoodle Story Tails
http://www.labradoodlestory.com

Melanie Ann Derwey of Gorgeous Doodles
http://gorgeousdoodles.com/

Amy Schuning of AKA's Doodles & Poodles
http://www.akasdoodlesandpoodles.com

Tera Mueller of Blessed Day Doodles
http://www.blesseddaydoodles.com/

Dixie Springer of Springville Labradoodles
http://www.springvillelabradoodles.com/

Babbie R. Holden of Royal Diamond Labradoodles
http://www.royaldiamondlabradoodles.com

Candace Trino of Moo Cow Labradoodles
http://www.MooCowLabradoodles.com

Jeanette & Mike Parker of Chesapeake Miniature
Labradoodles - E-mail: Packo7@shaw.ca

Sabrina Alstat of Sabrinas Labradoodles
http://sabrinaslabradoodles.com

Kristen Savery of Skyedoodles Labradoodles
http://www.Skyedoodles.com

Mardee Calkins of Texas Labradoodles
http://www.txlabradoodles.com/

Gayle Husfloen of North Country Australian Labradoodles
http://www.northcountrydoodles.com/

Acknowledgments

Julie Long of Faithful Doodles
http://www.faithfuldoodles.com

Brenda Van Deilen of Calypso Breeze Labradoodles
http://www.calypsobreezelabradoodles.com

Barb Gaffney of Gemstone Labradoodles
http://www.gemstonelabradoodles.ca/

Jacqui Carter-Davies of Jacarties Labradoodles (UK)
E-mail: carter-davies@supanet.com

Kiernon & Lisa Wagstaff - and Tia of course.

Photo Credit: Rochelle Woods of Spring Creek Labradoodles

Table of Contents

Table of Contents

Table of Contents

Table of Contents

Table of Contents

Table of Contents

Chapter 1 – Meet the Labradoodle

The Labradoodle doesn't suffer from a lack of positive press. Even if he did, he'd shake off the negative publicity, wag his tail and insist on a good game of fetch. The mix presents problems with achieving consistent results. Still, most Labradoodles are intelligent, happy and eager to please.

As an emerging breed, Labradoodles claim a kind of rock star status among hybrid dog enthusiasts, a fact both good and bad. The cross even comes with a good "back story." The idea to mate a Standard Poodle and a Labrador Retriever originated to meet a specific need. A blind woman in Hawaii whose husband suffered from allergies asked for a guide dog that wouldn't trigger his symptoms.

Initial attempts to match her with a working Poodle failed. The proposed solution was to cross a Poodle with a Labrador Retriever. The breeders hoped the puppies would have the

Lab's good nature and the Poodle's intelligence with a low-allergy coat.

The first litter produced puppies that did not trigger the husband's allergy symptoms. All three of the dogs exhibited higher-than-average intelligence and responded well to training. This led to further work in cultivating the new "designer breed" to realize the full potential of the hybrid cross.

As the breeding experiments continued, many of the puppies had no odor and minimal to no shedding. On the whole, the dogs were good natured and loyal. Even their size could match the kind of Poodle used for mating.

These early successes weren't as beneficial for the Labradoodle's future as you might suspect. Enthusiastic backyard breeders produced mixed dogs without an understanding of genetic consequences. Then the puppy mills realized the Labradoodle profit potential.

"Labradoodles" of even more questionable quality became common. Many showed serious genetic problems and iffy personalities. There's more to breeding dogs than letting nature take over. This fact becomes evident with crossbreeds from ill-matched mating pairs.

While Poodles are smart, they can also be territorial and stubborn. Both breeds exhibit hyperactivity and separation anxiety. If these factors aren't taken into account, the hybrid offspring can be the farthest thing from your "dream" dog.

If bred well, Labradoodles are "scary" smart. They have loving dispositions and play with impish pleasure. Breeders that test for genetic defects and develop targeted bloodlines should produce such dogs.

Labradoodle Breed History

Wally Conron, the puppy breeding manager for The Royal Guide Dogs in Victoria Australia, bred the first Labradoodles in 1988. He worked with the blind woman and her husband in Hawaii to create a hypoallergenic guide dog.

Conron sent hair and saliva samples from 33 different Poodles to the couple, but each caused an allergic reaction. In frustration, Conron decided to attempt a Poodle/Labrador Retriever mix.

Of the three puppies in the initial litter, one did not trigger an allergic reaction, but a different sort of problem evolved. The usual volunteers who walked and socialized guide dog puppies proved reluctant to take in the crossbreeds.

Conron went on Channel 9 in Melbourne to talk about a new breed of guide dog, which he christened the "Labradoodle." Willing puppy walkers jammed the phone lines and the Labradoodle "legend" was born.

Conron went on to breed Labradoodles with Labradoodles, a mix he called the "Double Doodle." Next, he bred those dogs to make what he called "Tri Doodles." Thirty-one dogs came out of his efforts, and twenty-nine worked as guide dogs.

As an offshoot of his project, two breeding and research centers formed in Australia in 1989:

- Rutland Manor Labradoodle Breeding and Research Centre in Darnum, Victoria.

- Tegan Park Labradoodle Breeding and Research Centre in Seaspray, Victoria.

The Tegan Park dogs were the first offered in three available sizes according to the type of Poodle used in the mating, these being miniature, medium and standard.

Considerable diversity in coat types proved to be one of the greatest challenges. Puppies with curlier coats showed the lowest allergy profile, but some molted by eight months. When the hair grew back, the new coat caused adverse reactions in people with allergies.

Consistency of texture proved problematic and the problem of uneven breed results continues to plague Labradoodles.

Photo Credit: Nicki Dana of Premiere Labradoodles

The Issue of Inconsistent Results

In a 2014 interview for *Psychology Today*, Wally Conron discussed his first crossbreeds. In spite of the early praise, Conron said results were unpredictable. The dog's appearance, working abilities and temperament varied to a large degree then and now.

One of the biggest areas of divergence is in coat appearance and texture. These include the:

- straight "hair" coat
- wavy, curly "fleece" coat
- curly, poodle-like "wool" coat

Many Labradoodles shed, and not all are hypoallergenic. In the interview, Conron describes his first litter and how the hypoallergenic misconception spread:

> "This is what gets up my nose, if you'll pardon the expression. When the pups were five months old, we sent clippings and saliva over to Hawaii to be tested with this woman's husband. Of the three pups, he was not allergic to one of them. In the next litter I had there were ten pups, but only three had non-allergenic coats. Now, people are breeding these dogs and selling them as non-allergenic, and they're not even testing them!"

Conron decries the widespread mixing of Poodles with all types of dogs. Backyard breeders and worse yet puppy mills promise the dogs will be hypoallergenic. Without correct genetic monitoring, such puppies suffer from health problems and behavioral issues.

Indeed, Dana Eckert of California Labradoodles says: "There is no such thing as a hypoallergenic dog of any breed. That is marketing hype. That being said, our dogs do very well with people with allergies. We've been breeding very consistent, allergy-friendly coats."

Unless you are dealing with an ethical breeder who verifies the health of his dogs, Conron advises caution. His own dogs are Labrador Retrievers, and he never bred Labradoodles beyond the thirty-one produced for The Royal Guide Dogs.

Australian, English or American Labradoodle?

Although originally bred from the Labrador and Poodle to produce the F1 Labradoodle Origin, in Australia both Rutland Manor and Tegan Park infused other breeds, including the American Cocker Spaniel, the English Cocker Spaniel and the Irish Water Spaniel. The term "Australian Labradoodle" now refers to dogs with some variation of those blood lines.
The broader term "Labradoodle," which I use in this book, means the dog is a cross between a Labrador Retriever and Poodle only.

Multigen Australian Labradoodle (or Multigenerational) are Labradoodles that result from the breeding of one Australian Labradoodle to another. The Multigens tend to have a more consistent coat and overall appearance due to the several generations of Australian Labradoodles behind them.

Australian Labradoodles (and Multigen) typically have a non-shedding coat as long as both parents are non-shedding, however, do be aware that there are recessive genes that can come into play that cause puppies from two non-shedding parents to end up with flat, short, retriever-type coats, and shedding coats. There is now a test for the IC gene (improper coat) to help determine which parents could produce puppies with the less-than-desirable shedding and flat coats. So, even though both parents may be non-shedding, if they both carry the IC gene, then they could have horribly shedding puppies.

Origin Labradoodles refer to a dog bred from only the Labrador and Poodle. They are not necessarily non-shedding.

Certain breeders in the USA will refer to their Labradoodles as "American Labradoodles" – in other words, American Kennel Club (AKC) recognized breeds, Labrador and Poodle. Other breeders in the USA will make clear they are selling the "Australian Labradoodle."

Likewise, in the United Kingdom, you will often see terms such as British Labradoodles, English Labradoodles or UK Labradoodles and once again these are Origin Labradoodles.

What is F1?

F1 means "first generation" and denotes a first-cross i.e. purebred Poodle to purebred Labrador Retriever. The results can be mixed and unpredictable. F1 Labradoodles typically have a sparse-hair to fleecy coat and can be very heavy shedders. The majority will shed less than a purebred Labrador, but it is the minority that end up low to no shed.

If you see the term F1B, this refers to "backcross" – in other words, an F1 Labradoodle backcrossed (bred) to a purebred Poodle.

An F1 Labradoodle is a 50% Lab and 50% Poodle, while an F1B Labradoodle is generally more Poodle, 75% Poodle and 25% Lab, helping with the shedding and allergy issues.

The term F2 would denote second generation and so forth.

Rochelle Woods of Spring Creek Labradoodles explains these percentages are not guaranteed: "When crossing a purebred Poodle with a purebred Lab, it does not always result in every puppy genetically being 50% of each breed. Genes don't work like that. Maybe on occasion you'd have an equal split, but not often. So, not only is the genetic makeup of the cross rarely 50%, but you also don't automatically have lower shedding puppies. I bred early generation and Australian generation the same length of time, and F1 litters are so varied I would never predict or promise anything to a family until I'd had a chance to physically assess a puppy as they were maturing. And even if they appeared to be possible low shedders, I wouldn't make any guarantees to anyone as it's too unpredictable in the F1 generation."

What is a 50/50?

This term refers to a Labradoodle that is 50% Labradoodle Origin and 50% Australian.

Physical Characteristics

The choice of Poodle in the mating pair determines the size of the resulting Labradoodle. The three variations are:

- Miniatures, 14-16 inches / 35.56-40.64 cm tall with a weight range of 15-25 lbs. / 6.8-11.3 kg

- Mediums, 17-20 inches / 43.18-50.80 cm tall with a weight range of 30-45 lbs. / 13.6-20.4 kg

- Standards, 21-24 inches / 53.34-60.96 cm tall with a weight range of 50-65 lbs. / 22.6-29.4 kg

Regardless of coat quality, the desired length is 4-6 inches / 10.16-15.24 cm. Coats vary in consistency and associated traits. It is not just the "look" of a coat that determines the coat type, but most importantly the texture of the coat:

- The straight "hair" coat is also known as flat or slick coat. These dogs shed and have the usual "doggy" odor. The hair coat occurs most often in first generation crosses.

- The "wool" coat is denser and can range from super curly, to not so curly. This variety does not shed and has no odor.

- The "fleece" coat is silky to the touch and may be straight to wavy. The consistency and appearance are like that of an Angora goat. This type of coat is odor free and does not shed.

Possible colors are: gold, apricot, caramel, chalk, black, red, café, cream, silver, chocolate, parchment and blue.

We have some great first-hand advice from UK breeder Jacqui Carter-Davies of Jacarties Labradoodles:

"In my experience, in the UK in particular, the hair coat Labradoodle is not as unpopular as you may think. Not everyone looking for a Labradoodle has allergy problems. Many new owners may have just lost their pedigree dog prematurely due to health problems (e.g. excessive line or in-breeding or problems with the particular breed) and their main aim is to buy a health-tested cross-breed dog from a larger gene pool, which will hopefully have a stronger immune system. For this reason, many people want an F1 Labradoodle as opposed to multi generation (there is less of a risk of Addisons, SA or PRA and recessive genes, etc.).

I always say to new owners there isn't a 'perfect dog' – you either vacuum or groom! The advantage of the scruffy, hair-coated Labradoodle is that you can take it to the beach, run through long grass/mud and not have to spend hours grooming when you get home; you haven't got the expense of regular clipping, etc., but they will shed (sometimes nearly as much as a Labrador!).

On the other hand, the fleecy/wool coats are suitable for people with allergies or who don't like vacuuming, but they are high maintenance – if you don't groom or have them clipped regularly, you will get punished with matts (especially behind the ears/collar/under the legs) and your beautiful long-haired dog will have to have a very severe clip at the groomers (which looks horrible!).

With regards to grooming Labradoodles, it is important to have a long-toothed comb as well as a brush. This helps remove hair from the roots and stop matts from developing.

As well as coat variations in a litter, you can also get size variations, particularly in F2 or backcross litters. Many breeders try to reduce the height/size of the standard

Labradoodles by mating them to a medium/miniature Labradoodle or miniature Poodle. By doing this, you can get throwbacks from the grandparents – one pup is as chunky as a Labrador or petite as a Miniature Poodle. It is important for prospective owners to be aware of this, as sadly many dogs end up in shelters just because they have 'grown too big.'

Unfortunately, it is over simplistic to say all hair coats are straight, as sometimes they can be curly, especially in a young puppy (they tend to go wavy when adult). Therefore, when choosing a puppy it is important to feel the coat as well as look at it. An allergy-friendly coat will be very soft, almost like velvet, whereas a hair coat will have a slightly coarser feel to it (sometimes almost a wiry feel).

When I first started breeding Labradoodles I let prospective owners visit when the puppies were 2+ weeks. However, I soon learnt that this was not a good idea, as the coats changed so much between 2 – 8 weeks. Some pups that had crinkly coats and showed all the signs of being curly, lost their waves by 8 weeks, and others that looked like little Labradors at 2 weeks developed lovely long wavy/fleecy coats by 8 weeks. I now don't let prospective buyers reserve a puppy before 4/5 weeks due to the coat changes (another big coat change is at 8+ months when the adult coat starts to come through, and they can go curlier or straighter; colour can change too, it usually goes lighter)."

Personality and Temperament

Labradoodles have a reputation for being intelligent, friendly dogs ideal for families. They are energetic and devoted companions. Both gentle and joyful, good training should curb their native exuberance. Labradoodles are easygoing and almost never show aggression.

Heredity, socialization and training affect temperament. The first two factors you can and should discuss with the breeder, but the second responsibility will rest with you. Socialization includes exposure to people, sights and sounds. This helps lay a foundation for a well-rounded, calm pet. Puppy "kindergarten," outings, walks and lots of human interaction also help.

The Labradoodle Puppy

Bringing a new puppy home is fun, even if the memories you're making include epic, puppy-generated messes! Young dogs are a huge responsibility no matter how much you love them, and they take a lot of work.

The first few weeks with any dog is an important phase that shapes the animal's adult behavior and temperament. Every new pet owner hopes to have a well-mannered, obedient and happy companion.

Puppy proofing, house training, grooming and feeding aren't the sole requirements. Critical socialization must also occur, including crate training. These measures prevent problem behaviors like whining, biting or jumping.

To achieve these goals, you must understand the breed with which you're working. That is not as easy with a hybrid or crossbred dog. The idea is that in combining two well-known and beloved breeds, you will get the best of both. The plan doesn't always work out in practical application. No absolute science exists to predict the traits in a crossbred dog.

Some general qualities are already associated with the Labradoodle. Breeders work to emphasize those desirable factors. Over time, these insights will solidify. For now, you must understand even with litters born to the same mother, personalities can be widely divergent.

The probability of getting a "good" dog is better if the dam and sire have excellent personalities. Still, every Labradoodle is a "person" in their own right.

With Other Pets

Most Labradoodles get along well with other pets thanks to selective breeding against aggression. The most problematic introduction will likely be with the family cat. Even if you can't engineer a total peace agreement with the resident feline, détente is an option. Don't force the animals to interact or to spend time together. When the puppy first arrives, put the little dog in its crate and allow the cat to check out the new arrival. Expect caution and vocal disapproval.

Supervise all interactions. Reinforce good behavior with treats and praise. Don't overreact to aggression or "trash talking." At this stage, the puppy is likely the one in need of rescuing from potential sharp-clawed swipes. Separate the animals with a firm "no" and try again later. Understand this can go on for several weeks until your pets reach some form of agreement whose terms only they will comprehend.

As for other kinds of animals, exercise reasonable caution and use your judgment i.e. never let any dog play with a rabbit.

With Children

Labradoodles make excellent companions for kids. Don't let a rambunctious puppy knock over and frighten smaller children. Those are the situations that create a lifelong fear of dogs. Most Labradoodles are gentle, loving and loyal. Good training will settle down an over-the-top, puppyish approach to the world.

Photo Credit: Julie Long of Faithful Doodles

Teach children to interact with all animals in a kind and proper way. Regardless, you should not leave a young child unsupervised with a dog, no matter how gentle or good natured. I don't think it is a good idea to have ANY dog with children under 3-4 years old. Prior to that they don't understand pinching, pulling and grabbing are not OK and the dog could bite in self-defense.

Wait until your children are 4-5 years of age when they are old enough to understand the Labradoodle's disposition and to respect his boundaries.

Male or Female?

The only time gender matters is if you are intending to breed the dog. Otherwise, focus on the individual Labradoodle's personality. In too many instances, people want female puppies because they assume they will be sweeter and gentler. No valid basis exists for this assumption. Don't use such a misconception to reject a male dog. The real determining factor in any dog's long-term behavior is the quality of its training in relation to its place in the family. Consistency in addressing bad behaviors before they start is crucial.

Female dogs coddled as puppies display more negative behavior and greater territoriality than males. Consider this factor when adopting a grown Labradoodle, especially in a rescue situation.

The greatest negative behaviors cited for male dogs are spraying and territorial urine marking. In the case of purebred adoptions, having the animal spayed or neutered is a condition of the purchase agreement.

Kennels make pet-quality animals available because they do not conform to the accepted breed standard. Such dogs are not suitable for exhibition or for use in a breeding program. Spaying and neutering under these circumstances protects the integrity of the kennel's bloodlines.

Since Labradoodles are not purebred dogs, this provision may or may not be part of a formal adoption agreement. Regardless, "best practice" advocates altering an animal before 6 months of age. Reduced hormone levels stop spraying in males and moodiness when a female is in heat. Both genders will also show less territorial aggression.

Beyond these considerations, Labradoodles are gender neutral. Either a male or a female can make a superb companion and family pet.

Puppy or Adult Dog?

People love puppies for all the obvious reasons. They are adorable, and the younger the dog is at adoption, the longer your time with your pet. At an average lifespan prediction of 12 to 14 years, Labradoodles are long lived in relation to their size.

If you do find an adult dog in need of adoption, longevity shouldn't be a "deal breaker" in welcoming the animal into your home.

I am a huge advocate of all animal rescue organizations. The numbers of homeless companion animals in need of adoption stands at shocking levels. To give one of these creatures a "forever" home is an enormous act of kindness. You will be saving a life.

In the vast majority of cases, Labradoodles are wonderful dogs. If your heart is set on one, I understand why. But if you are searching for a loyal four-legged friend of any breed, please do not rule out a shelter adoption.

Regardless of the dog you choose, please support rescue organizations. Such groups are always in need of donations and volunteer hours. When you do adopt a rescue dog, find out as much as possible about the dog's background and the reason for its surrender. With Labradoodles, you will rarely find one given up due to aggression.

Pets living with the elderly are often surrendered when their owner dies or goes into a care facility. Many are too energetic and exuberant for their owners regardless of age. Even more distressing, far too many homeless Labradoodles wind up in a shelter when they prove not to be hypoallergenic.

One or Two?

When you're sitting on the floor surrounded by frolicking Labradoodle puppies, your heart may tell you to go ahead and get two. Listen to your brain! Owning one dog is a serious commitment of time and money, but with two dogs, everything doubles: food, housebreaking, training, vet bills, boarding fees and time.

The good thing about Labradoodles is they adjust well to existing pets and to new animal companions. Introductions with puppies go well. Labradoodles are almost always thrilled with new companions, seeing them as playmates.

I would suggest pacing yourself. Start with one dog and put off a second adoption for the future.

The Need for Socialization

Any breed, no matter how well regarded for its temperament, can still develop bad habits and become obnoxious. Puppies should begin training at 10-12 weeks of age. (Finish the rabies, distemper and parvovirus vaccinations before exposing the puppy to other dogs.)

During formal training, understand you will be in "school" as much as your Labradoodle. Your job is "leader of the pack," a responsibility for which many humans are ill equipped without some in-class time of their own!

Famous Labradoodles and Their Owners

The following list of celebrity owners shows how far the dogs have wiggled their way into the spotlight!

- Jennifer Aniston
- David Baldacci
- Lance Bass
- Joe Biden
- Christie Brinkley
- Jeremy Clarkson
- Barbara Eden
- Henry Winkler
- Jeremy Irons
- Tiger Woods
- Neil Young
- Oliver Platt
- Graham Norton
- Lynn Hoffman
- Pam Krueger
- Julia Louis-Dreyfus

Photo Credit: Tera Mueller of Blessed Day Doodles

Chapter 2 - Labradoodle Dog Breed Standard

The Labradoodle is a hybrid dog and is not yet recognized by any official governing body within the dog fancy. The following breed standard (which I am reproducing verbatim with only paragraph breaks inserted for readability) is used by the Australian Labradoodle Club of America (ALCA).

It will give you an idea of what breeders who are actively working to standardize the breed currently consider the ideal qualities for a Labradoodle.

(Please note that this standard is for the Australian Labradoodle, which implies dogs with Cocker Spaniel DNA in their bloodline.)

General Appearance: The Australian Labradoodle should be athletic and graceful, yet compact with substance and medium boning. Joyful and energetic when free, soft and quiet when handled. They should approach people in a happy, friendly manner with eye-to-eye contact. Keen to learn and easy to train, they have a free-flowing wavy or curly coat that does not shed and is possibly non-allergenic.

Size: Sizes are still "somewhat inconsistent" with no definition between male and female at this time. Accurate prediction of size, even by an experienced breeder, is not expected at this time. Size is measured to the top of the shoulder blades (withers) while standing squarely on a level surface.

Much care is needed when breeding both the large and small dogs. Large dogs can suffer from rapid growth that can lead to structural problems. Soundness is of utmost importance. Over size is a major fault. Care must be taken to keep the miniature Australian Labradoodle a solid, athletic, robust dog.

The dwarfing of dogs can lead to many genetic and temperament disorders. Minimum size attention is of the utmost importance to maintain a healthy little dog. Most Australian Labradoodles will weigh more than their height reflects.

STANDARD: 21" TO 24"

The "Ideal" size for a standard female is 21 to 23 inches and for a male 22 to 24 inches. Weight range tends to be 50 to 65 pounds.

MEDIUM: 17" TO 20"

The "Ideal" size for a medium female is 17 to 19 inches and for a male 19 to 20 inches. Weight range tends to be 30 to 40 pounds.

MINIATURE: 14"TO 16"

The "Ideal" size for a miniature is 14 to 16 inches with no correlation between height and sex of the miniature Australian Labradoodle. Weight range tends to be 16 to 25 pounds.

Body: Height (to withers) to length (from sternum to point of buttock) should appear square and compact. Shoulders should have good angulation with firm elbows held close to the rib cage. Hindquarters should be of medium angulation with short, strong hocks. Top line should remain level with strong loin and level croup. Flanks should rise up from a brisket set just below the elbows, but should not be excessively deep. Ribs should be well sprung but not barreled. Overall, the dog should appear square, be balanced, athletic and with good muscling.

Movement: When trotting should be purposeful, strong and elastic, with good reach and drive, giving the appearance of "going somewhere." When happy, relaxed or at play will prance and skim the ground lightly. Excessive tightness in the hips will produce a stilted action and is considered a fault.

Tail: Set relatively high and preferred to be carried in a saber, can be carried below the topline or "gaily" above. Curled possum-type tails are undesirable.

Head: Sculptured, broad, well-defined eyebrows, medium stop, eyes set well apart, nose to stop slightly longer than stop to occiput. Foreface shorter than skull. The head should be clean and chiseled and fully coated as on the body, legs and tail. The muzzle is measured from the tip of the nose to the stop. The skull is measured from the occiput to the stop and does not include the muzzle.

Ears: Set moderately flat against the head, base should be level with the eye. Leather should be of medium thickness and when gently drawn forward should reach the top canine tooth. Ear leather reaching beyond the tip of nose is considered a severe fault. Ear canals should be free of excessive hair, and not thick and bulbous. When inquisitive and alert the ear set should rise to the top of the head. Thick/heavy ear leather is a fault.

Eyes: "Slightly" round, large and expressive, always offering eye-to-eye contact when engaged in activity with a human. Protruding or sunken eyes are a fault. Watery or tearful eyes are a fault. Wide, round or narrow, almond-shaped eyes are considered a fault.

Eye Color: Eye color should complement and blend with the face color. Black, Blue, Red, Dark Chocolate and Silver dogs must have dark brown eyes. All shades of Cafe', Milk Chocolate, Gold/Apricot, Cream and Chalk should have dark hazel to brown eyes if they have black pigment. Caramel and dogs with rose pigment may have either dark eyes or "ghost" eyes. Ghost is a hazel color range much the same as it is in humans. Flecking with different shades of hazel with green and a blue/green make this eye color quite unique. Ghost eyes must always remain soft in appearance. Cold, staring, expressionless appearance in all eye colors is a severe fault.

Teeth: Scissor bite only is acceptable, being neither undershot nor overshot. Miniatures must not have crowding teeth.

Nose: Large, square and fleshy. Pigment: Black or Rose. Pigment should be strong. Black pigment dogs must have dark brown eyes. Pink spots or patches on nose, lips, eye rims or pads are a fault. Dogs with rose pigment can have dark hazel, brown or ghost eyes. Eye rims should be rose as should nose, lips and pads. Pink spots or patches are a severe fault. Rose should be a rich liver color.

Neck: The firm, well-muscled neck should be moderately long, slightly arched and flow into the well-angled shoulders with no appearance of abruptness. The neck should not be coarse nor stumpy and should lend an air of elegance to the dog. A short, thick neck is a fault.

Photo Credit: Melanie Ann Derwey of Gorgeous Doodles

Color: Any solid color including Cafe' and Silver is preferred. Minimal white on the chest and toes is acceptable. Light, chalky coarse hairs (kemp) sprinkled through a dark coat is permissible but very undesirable.

Parti (patched) and Phantoms, though undesirable, are considered an acceptable color. Parti can be any color (except

Phantom) with white on face, head and/or body. Phantoms are any shading or two tone coloration, such as a Black dog with lower legs showing a soft toning of silver or gold or a dog born dark with a golden shading at the roots or a slight brindling effect. True pure solid colors with the exception of Silver and Cafe' are highly prized and are the ideal for the Australian Labradoodle.

It is normal that all colors may show bleaching and discoloration over the top coat. This is called sunning and is quite expected and acceptable, as the Australian Labradoodle is an active dog and often a service dog that enjoys the outdoors. Weather bleaching or sunning must not be penalized.

The Breed Standard of Excellence colors are:

Apricot/Gold, Red, Black, Silver and Blue - must have black pigment

Caramel, Chocolate, Cafe', Parchment and Lavender - must have rose pigment

Chalk (appears white but when compared to a true white it is a chalky white) - may have rose or black pigment

Cream and Apricot Cream (all shades and combinations of cream shades are acceptable) - may have rose or black pigment

Caramel: A rich Gold/Apricot very much the color of its namesake – caramel through to a deep red – must have rose pigment.

Red: A solid, even, rich red color, which should have no sprinkling of other colored fibers throughout the coat. A true

Red must not be lighter at the roots than at the tips of the coat. Red can fade somewhat with age, and senior dogs showing paling of coat should not be penalized.

Apricot/Gold: The color of a ripe apricot on the inside. A true Apricot must not be lighter at the roots than at the tips of the coat. It can come in varying shades and may fade as the dog grows older. Senior dogs should not be penalized for paling of coat color.

Blue: A dark to medium smoky Blue. Blue also belongs to the Rare Color Group. Blue dogs are born Black but will have Blue skin and undertonings at a young age. Any other color throughout the Blue is undesirable.

Silver: Born Black but will have more of a grey skin and will develop individual silver fibers at a young age. Silver dogs can take up to 3 years to color out and become a beautiful smoky grey through to a light iridescent platinum and varying shades in between at adulthood. Uneven layering of color in the silver is normal.

Chocolate: Dark and rich, born almost Black, they maintain a dark chocolate throughout their lifetime. Color should be even. Any other color throughout the Chocolate is highly undesirable. Chocolate belongs to the Rare Color Group.

Cafe': Born Milk Chocolate of varying shades, and have the same gene as the silver dogs, often taking up to 3 years to fully color out to multi shades of chocolate, silvery chocolate and silver throughout. When given plenty of time in the sunshine, they develop stunning highlights.

Lavender: A definite, even smoky lavender chocolate, giving almost pink/lilac appearance. Lavender dogs are born

Chocolate and can be difficult to distinguish at a young age. Any other color throughout the Lavender is highly undesirable. True Lavender belongs to the Rare Color Group.

Parchment: Born Milk Chocolate, will pale to a smoky, creamy beige. Paling usually starts from an early age, often as early as 6 weeks. As adults they can be mistaken for dark smoky Cream from a distance. Parchment belongs to the Rare Color Group.

COAT: Coat types are also still very sporadic, with many dogs showing a combination of multiple types. As the genetic values stabilize, we hope the "Ideal" coats are as follows:

Fleece: Length is usually around 5 inches long. The Fleece coat texture should be light and silky, quite similar to that of an Angora goat. Appearing "to contain a silky lanolin," the fleece coat can be from loosely waved, giving an almost straight appearance, to deeply waved. Kemp is often found around the eyes and topline. The absence of kemp is highly prized. Fleece coats rarely if ever shed. A slight shedding may occur and may be determined to the degree of wavy / curly. The less curly, the more chance of slight shedding.

During the age of 8-12 months, during the adolescent/maturing time, you will need to groom your fleece every week. After this "transition" period, the coat will settle down and maintenance will return to normal, requiring a comb out every 3-4 weeks. The fleece coat has been found to be allergy friendly.

Wool: Coats are denser to the feel, like a sheep's wool. The "Ideal" wool coat should "hang" in loose, hollow spirals. Most wool coats are still exhibiting a good texture but take the appearance of a Spring, not a Spiral. The sprung wool coat is not desirable. A thick (dense) coat is also not desirable. The Australian Labradoodle has a single coat.

Both the Fleece and the Wool coat should naturally grow in "staples" and be of a soft texture. Both the "Ideal" Fleece and Wool coats spin successfully. Hair coats (Hair texture that sheds) are a fault and are undesirable. It is extremely rare for a wool coat to shed, and is the preferred coat type for families with severe allergies.

To keep the wool coat long and flowing will require more maintenance. The wool coat looks beautiful cut shorter and is very easy to maintain. Grooming and a trim or clip three or four times a year is all that is required to keep the short wool coat looking great.

Chapter 3 – Getting Serious About Adoption

When you have moved past the stage of just "window shopping" for a dog and think you're pretty well settled on a Labradoodle, there are questions you need to ask yourself, and some basic education you should acquire.

Is a Labradoodle the Dog for You?

With a pedigreed dog, it's often easier to determine if a breed is or isn't a good fit in a given situation. My late father was, in his own way, a dog whisperer, and for the bulk of his life had nothing but "mutts," which is just a colloquialism for a crossbred dog.

It was not until his health began to fail that he became interested in Yorkshire Terriers because they exhibited the qualities of loyalty and feistiness he valued, but in a small, manageable "package."

Labradoodles are not, however, the product of random hybridization. They are, under the best of circumstances, a workable combination of qualities present in two well-documented breeds.

Under poor circumstances, they are the product of careless breeding and thus a bit of a genetic mess, a problem that can be sidestepped by careful acquisition from reputable sources.

The kinds of questions you want to ask yourself must, in so far as it is possible to do so, bridge all the potential ups and downs of owning this hybrid dog:

• Can your life accommodate the physical and emotional needs of a high energy breed that bonds deeply with its humans?

• Will you commit to grooming, which is fundamental to both health and appearance?

• You will not have the same level of consistency in choice that is the hallmark of purebred dogs purchased from breeders with carefully crafted bloodlines. The Labradoodle varies considerably in looks and types. Having said this, a knowledgeable breeder with experience is able to assess their puppies and give a really good idea of what the pup will look like as an adult based on having already produced that consistently for several generations.

The primary choices with which you will be confronted when you do begin to seriously look for a dog are "male or female" and "puppy or adult." While some people feel this simplifies the matter greatly, there are specific considerations relative to both of these choices.

Finding and Picking a Puppy

Typically, the first step in finding a specific type of puppy is tracking down a breeder. Thankfully in the case of the Labradoodle, the hybrid mix is becoming sufficiently well established, especially in the United States, Great Britain and Australia, with many reputable breeders to choose from.

Learn Basic Health Evaluation Tips

Before the "Aw Factor" kicks in and you are completely swept away by the cuteness of a Labradoodle puppy, familiarize yourself with the basic quick health checks you should make as you are playing with a young dog up for adoption.

- Although a puppy may be sleepy at first, the dog should wake up quickly and be both alert and energetic.

- The little dog should feel well fed in your hands, with some fat over the rib area.

- The coat should be shiny and healthy with no dandruff, bald patches or greasiness.

- The baby should walk and run easily and energetically, with no physical difficulty or impairment.

- The eyes should be bright and clear, with no sign of discharge or crustiness.

- Breathing should be quiet, with no excessive sneezing or coughing and no discharge or crust on the nostrils.

- Examine the area around the genitals to ensure there is no visible fecal collection or accumulation of pus.

- Test the dog's hearing by clapping your hands when the baby is looking away from you and judging the puppy's reaction.

- Test the vision by rolling a ball toward the dog, making sure the puppy appropriately notices and interacts with the object.

When you have educated yourself about what to look for in a healthy puppy, move on to visiting breeder websites or speaking over the phone to breeders in whose dogs you are interested. You want to arrive at a short list of potential breeders. Plan on visiting more than one before you make your decision.

Locating Breeders to Consider

If you do not have a national Labradoodle organization or club in your country, you will be faced with searching for breeder sites online. I will discuss evaluating breeders more fully in the chapter on buying a Labradoodle.

For now, know that your best option is to obtain a dog from a breeder that is clearly serious about their breeding program and displays this fact with copious information about their dogs, including lots and lots of pictures.

Finding advertisements for Labradoodles in local newspapers or similar publications is dicey at best. You may simply be dealing with a "backyard breeder," a well-meaning person who has allowed the mating of two dogs of different pedigrees. There is nothing inherently wrong with this situation, although I do strongly recommend that an independent veterinarian evaluate the puppy before you agree to adopt it.

All too often, however, if you go through the classified ads, you can stumble into a puppy mill, where dogs are being raised in deplorable conditions for profit only.

I am strongly in favor of being able to meet the parents and siblings and see for yourself the surroundings in which the dog was born and is being raised. If you are faced with having to travel to pick up your dog, it's a huge advantage to see recorded video footage or to do a live videoconference with the owner and the puppies.

It is far, far preferable to work with a breeder where you can verify the health of the parents and discuss with a knowledgeable breeder the potential for any congenital illnesses.

Responsible breeders are more than willing to give you all this information and more, and are actively interested in making sure their dogs go to good homes. If you don't get this "vibe" from someone selling you a dog, something is wrong.

Nowadays, many breeders are home based and their dogs live in the house as pets. Puppies are typically raised in the breeder's home as well. It's very common for Labradoodle breeders to use guardian homes for their breeding dogs. A guardian home is a permanent family for the dog. The breeder retains ownership of the dog during the years the dog is used for breeding, however, the dog lives with the guardian family. This arrangement is great for the dog because once retired from breeding, he/she is spayed/neutered and returned to its forever family. There is no need to re-home the dog after its breeding career has ended. There are still breeders who use kennels, but the number of home breeders is quite high.

The Timing of Your Adoption Matters

Be highly suspicious of any breeder that assures you they have dogs available at all times. It is normal, and a sign that you are working with a reputable breeder, when your name is placed on a waiting list.

(You may also be asked to place a small deposit to guarantee that you can adopt a puppy from a coming litter. Should you choose not to take one of the dogs, this money is generally refunded, but find out the terms of such a transaction in advance.)

Think about what's going on in your own life. Don't adopt a dog at a time when you have a huge commitment at work or there's a lot of disruption around an impending holiday.

Dogs, especially very smart ones like Labradoodles, thrive on routine. You want adequate time to bond with your new pet, and to help the little dog understand how his new world "runs."

Approximate Purchase Price

Targeting a price for an emerging breed like the Labradoodle can be difficult. You may well see newspaper listings for puppies as low as $50 / £31, but you have no way of guaranteeing the health of a dog bred in "backyard" circumstances. To be 100% certain you are getting the best quality dog whose genetics have been fully considered, expect to pay as much as $1500 / £934 (or more) for a Labrador/Poodle-only cross, depending on location and breeder.

Expect to pay $2500-$3000 for a Multigenerational Australian Labradoodle pet with pedigrees that go back to the founders of that breed (with the Spaniel infusions). A Multigenerational Australian Labradoodle purchased with health testing and breeding rights is likely priced about $10,000 with terms and conditions placed on it.

Pros and Cons of Owning a Labradoodle

Talking about pros and cons for any breed always draws me up a little short. It's a very subjective business since what one person may love in a breed, another person will not like at all.

I think Jack Russell Terriers are fantastically smart dogs, but they are also the drill sergeants of the canine world. I don't have any desire to give my life over to a dog that will run it at that level. My preference is for more laid-back breeds that value a good nap as highly as a rousing game of fetch.

People who love Labradoodles should be ready to talk about their good qualities as well as the challenges they pose for one overriding reason – a desire to see these very special animals go to the best home possible where they will be loved and appreciated.

Reasons to Adopt a Labradoodle

- Generally non-shedding with no odor.
- Low allergy profile.
- Good temperament / good family dogs.
- Good with children.
- Intelligent and trainable.

Reasons NOT to adopt a Labradoodle

- Not a recognized and standardized breed.
- No guarantees in regard to shedding and odor.
- No guarantees in regard to hypoallergenic status.
- Can be overly excitable and exuberant.
- A breed heavily targeted by "puppy mills."

Photo Credit: Julie Long of Faithful Doodles

Chapter 4 – Buying a Labradoodle

Breeders label pedigreed dogs as "pet" or "show" quality and set prices according to that standard. You won't face this issue with a hybrid dog like a Labradoodle. Still, reputable breeders don't just put a price on a dog and sell it to anyone who comes along.

Many of the same requirements for a pedigreed adoption will still apply in finding a Labradoodle. For instance, you may have to agree to spay or neuter the dog before it reaches six months of age. You should also receive standard health guarantees, as well as genetic information and any existing medical records.

If you are adopting from a "backyard" breeder, these terms will be absent. This doesn't mean you'll be getting a "bad" dog. You do, however, take a greater risk for potential problems in the areas of health, genetic quality and behavior.

How to Choose a Breeder

Try finding a local breeder or one in reasonable traveling distance. Even if you find a Labradoodle breeder online, visit the breeder at least once before adopting. Plan on picking the animal up in person if possible.

Be suspicious of any breeder unwilling to allow such a visit or one who doesn't want to show you around their facilities. You don't want to interact with just one puppy. You should be meeting the parent(s) and the entire litter.

It's important to get a sense of how the dogs live and their level of care. When you talk to the breeder, information should flow in both directions. The owner should discuss both the positives and negatives of the Labradoodle cross.

Tracy A. Wynn of Desert Winds Labradoodles says: "Breeders who ship puppies are not necessarily bad breeders or puppy mills, but the buyer must do thorough homework and research into the breeder. We ship puppies, but are a small in-home breeder that does extensive health testing above and beyond what is required to achieve Gold Paw status with the ALAA, which we are a member of as well as the ALCA. We crate train our puppies and take them for car rides and expose them to noise, so that by the time they are 8 weeks of age, they are sleeping at night at least 6 hours straight without a need to go potty and remain dry in their crates. Therefore, they handle their short direct plane rides with ease. Puppy buyers are always welcome in our home to meet our dogs and puppies but we do also sell to people who are unable to travel to us to meet us or the dogs in person. We have live webcams on our litters for the families out of state to watch how they are cared for 24/7."

What to Expect from a Good Breeder

Responsible breeders help you select a puppy. They place the long-term welfare of the dog front and center. The breeder should show interest in your life and ask questions about your schedule, family and other pets.

This is not nosiness. Breeders are Labradoodle experts. They should try to judge the correctness of the placement. Breeders who aren't interested in what kind of home the dog will have are suspect.

The Breeder Should Provide the Following

Since Labradoodles are not a recognized breed, adoptions may be more informal. In the best cases, the transaction still includes the following components:

- The *contract of sale* details both party's responsibilities. It also explains the transfer of paperwork and records.

- The *information packet* offers feeding, training and exercise advice. It also recommends standard procedures like worming and vaccinations.

- The *description of ancestry* includes the names and types of Labrador and Poodle used in breeding.

- *Health records* detail medical procedures, including vaccination records, and disclose potential genetic issues.

- The breeder should *guarantee the puppy's health* at the time of adoption. In pedigreed adoptions, purchasers must confirm this fact with a vet within a set period of time. Even if a health evaluation isn't required, it's a good precaution.

Warning Signs of a Bad Breeder

Always be alert to key warning signs like:

- Breeders who tell you it is not necessary for you to visit the kennels in person.

- Assertions that you can buy a puppy sight unseen with confidence.

- Breeders who will allow you to come to their home but who will not show you where the dogs live.

- Homes or kennels keeping dogs in overcrowded conditions where the animals seem nervous and apprehensive.

- Situations in which you are not allowed to meet at least one of the puppy's parents.

- Sellers who can't produce health information or that say they will provide the records later.

- No health guarantee and no discussion of what happens if the puppy does fall ill, including a potential refund.

- Refusal to provide a signed bill of sale or vague promises to forward one later.

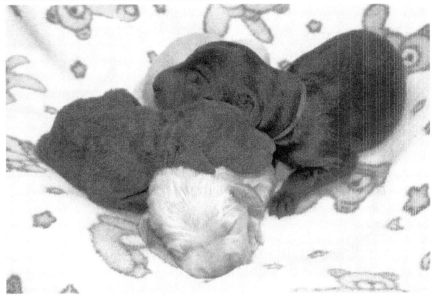

Photo Credit: Nicki Dana of Premiere Labradoodles

Avoiding Scam Puppy Sales

No one wants to support a puppy mill. Such operations exist for profit only. They crank out the greatest number of litters possible with an eye toward nothing but the bottom line.

The care the dogs receive ranges from deplorable to non-existent. Inbreeding is standard, leading to genetic abnormalities, wide-ranging health problems and short lifespans.

The Internet is, unfortunately, a ripe advertising ground for puppy mills, as are pet shops. If you can't afford to buy from a reputable breeder, consider a shelter or rescue adoption. Even if you can't be 100% certain you're getting a Labradoodle, you are adopting an animal in need.

Some scammers will advertise a single puppy on the free-to-advertise websites and get you to pay a "deposit" over the

Internet. They leave the advert open long enough to rake in a number of deposits, then remove the ad and create a new one from a different location.

Many breeders are not what they appear to be. They often have multiple websites, phone numbers and email addresses for each breed they sell. All of their dogs may not be at the same location, or they work together with friends or family to help hide these facts. A good website is easy to create. Do some snooping around using Google, online white pages, GIS, tax, maps, etc., and you might be surprised at what you find out.

Puppy mills see profit in the growing popularity of "designer dogs," but give no thought to breeding integrity. Again, if you can't:

- visit the home or kennel where the puppies were born
- meet the parents
- inspect the facilities
- and receive some genetic and health information

...something is wrong.

Best Age to Purchase a Puppy

A Labradoodle puppy needs time to learn important life skills from the mother dog, including eating solid food and grooming themselves.

For the first month of a puppy's life, they will be on a mother's milk-only diet. Once the puppy's teeth begin to appear, they will start to be weaned from mother's milk, and by the age of 8 weeks should be completely weaned and eating just puppy food.

Puppies generally leave between 7-9 weeks and are usually

weaned before they receive their first vaccines. Some moms will continue to nurse despite the puppy being on solid food.

In some cases, the mom is too overwhelmed with the size of the pups and the size of the litter, and she avoids them. This occurs as early as 6 weeks old and can result in bad behaviors as the puppies interact with each other. Their roughhouse playing becomes more and more imprinted on them, and families could struggle to teach the puppy not to play with children as they do with their litter mates.

Trainers highly recommend training and bonding should begin with their new families by 8-10 weeks. In addition, pups need to be highly socialized between 8-12 weeks with new people, new experiences and places. This time period is very crucial in developing a well-rounded pup.

With vet approval being required in some states, a breeder can place pups a little earlier than 8 weeks, if the puppies show signs of being properly weaned and being socially mature enough. In fact, every mommy/litter experience will be a little different. It's up to the breeder to evaluate each litter individually and determine the best timing for release, based primarily on proper weaning and maturity.

How to Pick a Puppy?

My standard strategy in selecting a pup has always been to sit a little apart from a litter and let one of the dogs come to me. My late father was, in his own way, a "dog whisperer." He taught me this trick for picking puppies, and it's never let me down. I've had dogs in my life since childhood and enjoyed a special connection with them all. I will say that often the dog that comes to me isn't the one I might have chosen — but I still consistently rely on this method. Having said this, I am very experienced in understanding the body language and behavior of dogs.

Beyond that, I suggest that you interact with your dog with a clear understanding that each one is an individual with unique traits. It is not so much a matter of learning about all Labradoodles, but rather of learning about YOUR Labradoodle dog.

You will want to choose a puppy with a friendly, easy-going temperament, and your breeder should be able to help you with your selection, as there are many factors to be considered. It is important to rely on the breeder's assessment and input regarding each puppy; the breeder has raised them and assessed them. They can match a puppy that suits your needs, as well as determining if you are a good fit for the puppy. Also ask the breeder about the temperament and personalities of the puppy's parents and if they have socialized the puppies.

Always be certain to ask if a Labradoodle puppy you are interested in has displayed any signs of aggression or fear, because if this is happening at such an early age, you may experience behavioral troubles as the puppy becomes older.

Some people immediately turn into mush when they come face to face with cute little puppies, and still others become very emotional when choosing a puppy, which can lead to being attracted to those who display extremes in behavior.

Check Puppy Social Skills

When choosing a puppy out of a litter, look for one that is friendly and outgoing, rather than one who is overly aggressive or fearful.

Puppies who demonstrate good social skills with their litter mates are much more likely to develop into easy-going, happy adult dogs that play well with others.

Photo Credit: Candace Trino of Moo Cow Labradoodles

Observe all the puppies together and take notice:

Which puppies are comfortable both on top and on the bottom when play fighting and wrestling with their litter mates, and which puppies seem to only like being on top?

Which puppies try to keep the toys away from the other puppies, and which puppies share?

Which puppies seem to like the company of their litter mates, and which ones seem to be loners?

Puppies that ease up or stop rough play when another puppy yelps or cries are more likely to respond appropriately when they play too roughly as adults.

Is the puppy sociable with humans? If they will not come to you, or they display fear toward strangers, this could develop into a problem later in their life.

Is the puppy relaxed about being handled? If they are not, they may become difficult with adults and children during daily interactions, during grooming or visits to the veterinarian's office.

Check Puppy's Health

Ask to see veterinarian reports to satisfy yourself that the puppy is as healthy as possible. Before making your final pick of the litter, check for general signs of good health, including the following:

1.   Breathing: will be quiet, without coughing or sneezing, and there will be no crusting or discharge around their nostrils.
2.   Body: will look round and well-fed, with an obvious layer of fat over their rib cage.
3.   Coat: will be soft, with no dandruff or bald spots.
4.   Energy: a well-rested puppy should be alert and energetic.
5.   Hearing: a puppy should react if you clap your hands behind their head.
6.   Genitals: no discharge visible in or around their genital or anal region.
7.   Mobility: they will walk and run normally, without wobbling, limping or seeming to be stiff or sore.
8.   Vision: bright, clear eyes, with no crust or discharge.

Breeder Advice

This advice for buying an Australian Labradoodle comes from Dana Eckert of California Labradoodles:

"Buyers should look for breeders that do extensive health testing on their breeding stock.

They should choose a breeder that breeds toward the breed standard as set by the ALAA and the ALCA – or breeders who go above and beyond what is required by the Labradoodle Associations.

The ALAA awards gold and silver paws for health testing and requires these tests be up to date and current. Breeders are required to agree to both yearly and random audits. Buyers should pay attention to this.

Buyers should also pick a breeder who studies the temperament of their puppies over time, not in a single moment. There is much more to picking a pup than selecting the pup that comes to you. When you come to visit, the quiet sleepy puppy may have just run around for two hours, and the alert pup may have just woke up from a nap. Temperament is our most important criteria in placing our pups.

People should pay attention to the kind of socialization the breeder does with their babies before they go to their new homes. We expose our pups to as many new sights and sounds as possible. I take them driving in the car, to my kids football games, to the grocery store, to the vet. They live with us in our home so have all the sights and sounds of an active family life and three loving boys. We expose them to as many people as possible.

And lastly, look at the environment in which the dogs are raised. Our three dogs live with us in our home. We are not a kennel. Two of our three Australian Labradoodles are spayed and retired, and are our personal pets. We only have one breeding dog here. All the rest of our dogs live in carefully selected guardian homes. That way, each and every dog in our breeding program is a loved and important member of their own family and gets all the individual attention and pampering they need. And that ensures that we also have lots of love and attention to go around whenever our care family girls or boys come for a visit."

Photo Credit: Candace Trino of Moo Cow Labradoodles

Chapter 5 – Caring for Your New Puppy

All puppies are forces of nature. That's especially true for an exuberant, sweet, curious, happy Labradoodle! They are little dogs that can get in big trouble before you even know what's happened. The first job ahead of you – and I do mean *before* you bring your new pet home – is to puppy proof the house!

Photo Credit: Candace Trino of Moo Cow Labradoodles

The Fundamentals of Puppy Proofing

Think of a puppy as a bright toddler with four legs. Get yourself in the mindset that you're bringing a baby genius home, and try to think like a puppy. Every nook and cranny invites exploration. A puppy's inquisitive nose goes into every crevice. Every discovery is then chewed, swallowed – or both!

Household Poisons

Although most people think dogs are carnivores, man's best friend is an omnivore. A dog, especially a young one, will eat pretty much anything, often gulping something down with no forethought.

Take a complete inventory of the areas to which the dog will have access. Remove all lurking poisonous dangers from cabinets and shelves. Get everything up and out of the dog's reach. Pay special attention to:

- cleaning products
- insecticides
- mothballs
- fertilizers
- antifreeze

If you are not sure about any item, assume it's poisonous and remove it.

Looking Through Your Puppy's Eyes

Get down on the floor and have a look around from puppy level. Your new furry Einstein will spot anything that catches your attention and many things that don't!

Do not leave any dangling electrical cords, drapery pulls or even loose scraps of wallpaper. Look for forgotten items that have gotten wedged behind cushions or kicked under the furniture. Don't let anything stay out that is a potential choking hazard.

Tie up anything that could be a "topple" danger. A coaxial cable may look boring to you, but in the mouth of a determined little dog, it could bring a heavy television set crashing down. Cord minders and electrical ties are your friends!

Remove stuffed items and pillows, and cover the legs of prized pieces of furniture against chewing. Take anything out of the room that even looks like it *might* be a toy. Think I'm kidding? Go online and do a Google image search for "dog chewed cell phone" and shudder at what you will see.

Plant Dangers, Inside and Out

The list of indoor and outdoor plants that are a toxic risk to dogs is long and includes many surprises. You may know that apricot and peach pits are poisonous to canines, but what about spinach and tomato vines?

The American Society for the Prevention of Cruelty to Animals has created a large reference list of plants for dog owners here:

http://www.aspca.org/pet-care/animal-poison-control/toxic-and-non-toxic-plants

Go through the list and remove any plants from your home that might make your puppy sick. Don't think for a minute that your dog will leave such items alone. He won't!

Preparing for the Homecoming

Before you bring your new puppy home, buy an appropriate travel crate and a wire crate for home use. Since the home crate will also be an important tool in housebreaking, the size of the unit is important.

Many pet owners want to get a crate large enough for the puppy to "grow into" in the interest of saving money. When you are housebreaking a dog, you are working with the principle that the animal will not soil its own "den." If you buy a huge crate for a small dog, the puppy is likely to pick a corner as the "bathroom," thus setting back his training.

Crates are rated by the size of the dog in pounds / kilograms:

- For a medium Labradoodle (40 lbs. / 18.14 kg), the crate should be 36" X 25" X 27" / 91.44 cm x 63.5 cm x 68.58 cm.

- For a small Labradoodle (30 lbs. / 13.6 kg), choose a crate that is 32" X 22.5" X 24" / 81.28 cm x 57.15 cm x 60.96.

Photo Credit: Candace Trino of Moo Cow Labradoodles

Put one or two puppy-safe chew toys in the crate for the ride home, along with a recently worn article of clothing. You want the dog to learn your scent. Be sure to fasten the seat belt over the crate.

Talk to the breeder to ensure the dog has not eaten recently. Take the puppy out to do its business before putting it in the crate. Expect whining and crying. Don't give in! Leave the dog in the crate! It's far safer for the puppy to ride there than to be in someone's lap.

If you are driving a considerable distance, some breeders will recommend mild sedation. If you are uncomfortable with this idea, take someone with you to sit next to the crate and comfort the puppy.

Don't overload the dog's senses with too many people. No matter how excited the kids may be at the prospect of a new puppy, leave the children back at the house. The trip home needs to be calm and quiet.

As soon as you arrive home, take the puppy to a patch of grass outside to relieve himself. Immediately begin encouraging him for doing so. Dogs are pack animals with an innate desire to please their "leader." Positive and consistent praise is an important part of housebreaking.

Even a gregarious dog like a Labradoodle will feel nervous in new surroundings away from its mother and litter mates. Stick with the usual feeding schedule, and use the same kind of food that the dog has been receiving at the breeders.

Create a designated "puppy safe" area in the house, and let the puppy explore on its own. Don't isolate the little dog, but don't overwhelm it either. Resist the urge to pick up the puppy every time it cries.

Give the dog soft pieces of worn clothing to further familiarize him with your scent. Leave a radio playing at a low volume for "company." At night, you may opt to give the baby a well-wrapped warm water bottle, but put the dog in its crate and do not bring it to bed with you.

I realize that last bit may sound all but impossible, but if you want a crate-trained dog, you have to start from day one. It's much, much harder to get a dog used to sleeping overnight in his crate after any time in the bed with you.

The Importance of the Crate

The crate plays an important role in your dog's life. Don't think of its use as "imprisoning" your Labradoodle. The dog sees the crate as a den and will retreat to it for safety and security. Dogs often go to their crates just to enjoy quiet time.

When you accustom your dog to a crate as a puppy, you get ahead of issues of separation anxiety and prepare your pet to do well with travel. The crate also plays an important role in housebreaking, a topic we will discuss shortly.

Never rush crate training. Don't lose your temper or show frustration. The Labradoodle must go into the crate on its own. Begin by leaving the door open. Tie it in place so it does not slam shut on accident. Give your puppy a treat each time he goes inside. Reinforce his good behavior with verbal praise.

Never use the crate as punishment. Proper use of the crate gives both you and your dog peace of mind.

Go Slow with the Children

If you have children, talk to them before the puppy arrives. Explain that the little dog will be nervous and scared being away from its mother and old home. The initial transition is important. Supervise all interactions for everyone's safety and comfort.

Help children understand how to handle the puppy and to carry it safely. Limit playtime until everyone gets to know each other. In just a matter of days, your Labradoodle puppy will be romping with your kids.

Introductions with Other Pets

Introductions with other pets, especially with cats, often boil down to matters of territoriality. All dogs, by nature, defend their territory against intruders. This instinct is strong in Poodles and often surfaces in Labradoodles.

Don't let a Labradoodle puppy and a cat meet face-to-face without some preparation. Create a neutral and controlled interaction under a closed bathroom door first. Since cats are "weaponized" with an array of razor sharp claws, Fluffy can quickly put a puppy in his place. Of course, you want to oversee the first "in-person" meeting, but don't overreact. Let the animals sort it out.

With other dogs in the house, you may want a more hands-on approach to the first "meet and greet." Always have two people present to control each dog. Make the introduction in a place that the older dog does not regard as "his." Even if the two dogs are going to be living in the same house, let them meet in neutral territory.

Keep your tone and demeanor calm, friendly and happy. Let the dogs conduct the usual "sniff test," but don't let it go on for too long. Either dog may consider lengthy sniffing to be aggression. Puppies may not yet understand the behavior of an adult dog and can be absolute little pests.

If this is what is going on, do not scold the older dog for issuing a warning snarl or growl. A well-socialized older dog won't be displaying aggression under such circumstances. He's just putting junior in his place and establishing the hierarchy of the pack.

Photo Credit: Becky & Jim Roth of Southern Cross Australian Labradoodles

Be careful when you bring a new dog into the house not to neglect the older dog. Also be sure to spend time with him away from the puppy to assure your existing pet that your bond with him is strong and intact.

Exercise caution at mealtimes. Feed your pets in separate bowls so there is no perceived competition for food. (This is also a good policy to follow when introducing your puppy to the family cat.)

Common Mistakes to Avoid

Never pick your Labradoodle puppy up if they are showing fear or aggression toward an object, other dog or person, because this will be rewarding them for unbalanced behavior.

If they are doing something you do not want them to continue, your puppy needs to be gently corrected by you with firm and calm energy, so that they learn not to react with fear or aggression. When the mum of the litter tells her puppies off, she will use a deep noise with strong eye contact, until the puppy quickly realize it is doing something naughty.

Don't play the "hand" game, where you slide the puppy across the floor with your hands because it's amusing to see a little ball of fur excitedly run back across the floor for another go.

This sort of "game" will teach your puppy to disrespect you as their leader in two different ways — first, because this "game" teaches them that humans are their play toys, and secondly, this type of "game" teaches them that humans are a source of excitement.

When your Labradoodle puppy is teething, they will naturally want to chew on everything within reach, and this will include you. As cute as you might think it is when they are young puppies, this is not an acceptable behavior, and you need to gently, but firmly, discourage the habit, just like a mother dog does to her puppies when they need to be weaned.

Always praise your puppy when they stop inappropriate behavior, as this is the beginning of teaching them to understand rules and boundaries. Often we humans are quick to discipline a puppy or dog for inappropriate behavior, but we forget to praise them for their good behavior.

Don't treat your Labradoodle like a small, furry human. When people try to turn dogs into people, this can cause them much stress and confusion that could lead to behavioral problems.

A well-behaved Labradoodle thrives on rules and boundaries, and when they understand that there is no question you are their leader and they are your follower, they will live a contented, happy and stress-free life.

Dogs are a different species with different rules; for example, they do not naturally cuddle, and they need to learn to be stroked and cuddled by humans. Therefore, be careful when approaching a dog for the first time and being overly expressive with your hands. The safest areas to touch are the back and chest — avoid patting on the head and touching the ears.

Many people will assume that a dog that is yawning is tired — this is often a misinterpretation, and instead it is signaling your dog is uncomfortable and nervous about a situation.

Be careful when staring at dogs, because this is one of the ways in which they threaten each other. This body language can make them feel distinctly uneasy.

What Can I Do to Make My Labradoodle Love Me?

From the moment you bring your Labradoodle dog home, every minute you spend with him is an opportunity to bond. The earlier you start working with your dog, the more quickly that bond will grow and the closer you and your Labradoodle will become.

While simply spending time with your Labradoodle will encourage the growth of that bond, there are a few things you can do to purposefully build your bond with your dog. Some of these things include:

- Taking your Labradoodle for daily walks during which

you frequently stop to pet and talk to your dog.

•   Engaging your Labradoodle in games like fetch and hide-and-seek to encourage interaction.

•   Interacting with your dog through daily training sessions – teach your dog to pay attention when you say his name.

•   Being calm and consistent when training your dog – always use positive reinforcement rather than punishment.

•   Spending as much time with your Labradoodle as possible, even if it means simply keeping the dog in the room with you while you cook dinner or pay bills.

Photo Credit: Barbara Dearaujo of Dreamydoodles Northwest

Puppy Nutrition

As dogs age, they thrive on a graduated program of nutrition. At age four months and less, puppies should get four small meals a day. From age 4-8 months, three meals per day are appropriate. From 8 months on, feed your pet twice a day.

Set feeding times make housebreaking easier. Don't free feed your Labradoodle until it is grown. Labrador Retrievers have a reputation for gaining weight, and this tendency passes on to Labradoodles. You can leave dry food out for a grown dog, but if your pet starts to become obese, return to set meal times.

Begin feeding your puppy by putting the food down for 10-20 minutes. If the dog doesn't eat, or only eats part of the serving, still take the bowl up. Don't give the dog more until the next scheduled feeding.

To give your puppy a good start in life, rely on high quality, premium dry puppy food. If possible, replicate the puppy's existing diet. A sudden dietary switch can cause gastrointestinal upset. Maintain the dog's existing routine if practical.

Before buying any dog food, read the label. The first listed ingredients should be meat, fishmeal or whole grains. Foods with large amounts of fillers like cornmeal or meat by-products have a low nutritional value. They fill your dog up, but don't give him the necessary range of vitamins and minerals, and they increase daily waste produced.

Wet foods are not appropriate for most growing dogs. They do not offer a good nutritional balance, and they are often upsetting to the stomach. Additionally, it's much harder to control portions with wet food, leading to young dogs being over or under fed.

Controlling portions is important. Give your dog the amount stipulated on the food packaging for his weight and age, and nothing more.

Invest in weighted food and water bowls made out of stainless steel. The weights prevent the mess of "tip overs," and the material is much easier to clean than plastic. It does not hold odors or harbor bacteria.

Bowls in a stand that create an elevated feeding surface are also a good idea. Make sure your young dog can reach the food and water. Stainless steel bowl sets retail for less than $25 / £14.87.

Adult Nutrition

The same basic nutritional guidelines apply to adult Labradoodles. Always start with a high-quality, premium food. If possible, stay in the same product line the puppy received at the breeders. Graduated product lines help owners to create feeding programs that ensure nutritional consistency.

This approach allows you to transition your Labradoodle away from puppy food to an adult mixture, and in time to a senior formula. This removes the guesswork from nutritional management.

Say No to Table Scraps!

Dogs don't make it easy to say no when they beg at the table. If you let a Labradoodle puppy have so much as that first bite, you've created a little monster – and one with an unhealthy habit.

(Even acceptable treats formulated for dogs should never comprise more than 5% of a dog's daily food intake.)

Table scraps contributes to weight problems, and many human foods are toxic to dogs. Dangerous items include, but are not limited to:

- Chocolate
- Raisins
- Alcohol
- Human vitamins (especially those with iron)
- Mushrooms
- Onions and garlic
- Walnuts
- Macadamia nuts
- Raw fish
- Raw pork
- Raw chicken

If you give your puppy a bone, watch him. Use only bones that are too large to choke on, and take the item away at the first sign of splintering. Commercial chew toys rated "puppy safe" are a much better option.

Your Puppy's First Lessons

Don't give a young dog full run of the house before it is house trained. Keep your new pet confined to a designated area behind a baby gate. This protects your home and possessions and keeps the dog safe from hazards like staircases.

Depending on the size and configuration, baby gates retail from $25-$100 / £14.87-£59.46. During those times when you are not home to supervise the puppy, crate your pet.

Photo Credit: Karen Elliott of Rocky Mountain Labradoodles

Housebreaking

Crate training and housebreaking go hand in hand. Labradoodles, like all dogs, come to see their crate as their den. They will hold their need to urinate or defecate while they are inside. Any time you leave the house, you should crate your pet, immediately taking the dog out upon your return.

Establishing and maintaining a daily routine also helps your dog in this respect. Feed your pet at the same time each day, taking him out afterwards. The feeding schedule dictates the frequency of "relief" breaks. Trips "out" will also decrease as the dog ages.

Don't be rigid in holding your puppy to this standard. Puppies have less control over their bladder and bowel movements than adult dogs. They need to go out more often, especially after they've been active or gotten excited.

On average, adult dogs go out 3-4 times a day: when they wake up, within an hour of eating and right before bedtime. With puppies, don't wait more than 15 minutes after a meal.

Praise your pet with the same phrases to encourage and reinforce good elimination habits. NEVER punish a dog for having an accident. There is no association in the dog's mind with the punishment and the incident. He'll have an uncomfortable awareness that he's done *something* to make you unhappy, but he won't know what.

Of course, if you catch your dog in the act of eliminating in the house, you can and should say "bad dog," but then let the matter go. Clean up the accident using an enzymatic cleaner to eradicate the odor and return to the dog's normal routine. Nature's Miracle Stain and Odor Removal is an excellent product and is affordable at $5 / £2.97 per 32 ounce / 0.9 liter bottle.

Marking Territory

Both male and female dogs with intact reproductive systems mark territory by urinating. This is most often an outdoor behavior, but can happen inside if the dog is upset.

Again, use an enzymatic cleaner to remove the odor and minimize the attractiveness of the location to the dog. Territory marking is especially prevalent in intact males. The obvious long-term solution is to have the dog neutered.

Marking territory is not a consequence of poor house training. The behavior can be seen in dogs that would otherwise never "go" in the house. It stems from completely different urges and reactions.

Dealing with Separation Anxiety

Separation anxiety manifests in a variety of ways, ranging from vocalizations to nervous chewing. Dogs that are otherwise well trained may urinate or defecate in the house. These behaviors begin when your dog recognizes signs that you are leaving. Triggers include picking up a set of car keys or putting on a coat. The dog may start to follow you around the house trying to get your attention, jumping up on you or otherwise trying to touch you.

It is imperative that you understand when you adopt a Labradoodle that they are companion dogs. They must have time to connect and be with their humans. You are the center of your dog's world. The behavior that a dog exhibits when it has separation anxiety is not a case of the animal being "bad." The poor thing experiences real distress and loneliness.

The purpose of crate training is not to punish or imprison a dog. It is not a cruel or repressive measure. The crate is the dog's "safe place," and is a great coping mechanism for breeds with separation anxiety issues. You are not being mean or cruel teaching your dog to stay in a crate when you are away, you are *helping* your pet to cope.

Grooming

Do not allow yourself to get caught in the "my Labradoodle doesn't like it" trap, which is an excuse many owners will use to avoid regular grooming sessions. When you allow your dog to dictate whether they will permit a grooming session, you are setting a dangerous precedent.

Once you have bonded with your dog, they love to be tickled, rubbed and scratched in certain favorite places. This is why grooming is a great source of pleasure and a way to bond with your pet.

The frequency of your dog's grooming schedule will depend on the length of his coat. Get your Labradoodle used to brushing at home to help prevent tangles and to keep his coat healthy.

- Bristle brushes work well with all coats from long to short. They remove dirt and debris and distribute natural oils throughout the coat.
- Wire-pin brushes are for medium to long, curly or wooly coats and look like a series of pins stuck in a raised base.
- Slicker brushes are excellent for smoothing and detangling, especially for long hair.

(Note you can often find combination, two-headed brushes. They'll save you a little money and make your grooming sessions easier.)

Each of these types of brush costs less than $15 / £9 and often less than $10 / £6.

Photo Credit: Kristen Savery of Skyedoodles Labradoodles

Grooming/brushing sessions are an excellent opportunity to examine your dog's skin. Look for any growths, lumps, bumps or wounds. Also have a good look at his ears, eyes and mouth.

As Poodles have hairy ears and Labradors tend to have quite waxy ears (not a great combination!), it is important to check the ears regularly and pluck out any excess hair, otherwise wax can build up and the ears can become prone to infection.

Labradoodles have an increased issue with their ears, since the hair is thick and grows inside the ear canal and the ear is covered by floppy ears.

Vigilant prevention is the hallmark of good healthcare for all companion animals. Watch for any discharge from the eyes or ears, as well accumulated debris in the ear canal and a foul or yeasty odor. (This is a sign of parasitical mite activity.)

If you bathe your dog at home between clippings, do not get your pet's head and ears wet. Clean the dog's head and face with a warm, wet washcloth only. Rinse your dog's coat with clean, fresh water to remove all residue. Towel your pet dry and make sure he doesn't get chilled.

Although some brave owners may clip their dogs at home, I recommend using the services of a professional. The risk of injuring your dog with a cutting tool is too great, in my opinion. Most groomers are quite reasonable, charging in a range of $25-$50 / £15-£30 per session.

Nail Trimming

Coat maintenance is not the only grooming chore necessary to keep your Labradoodle in good shape. Even dogs that walk on asphalt or other rough surfaces often will need to have their nails trimmed from time to time.

If your pet is agreeable, this is a job you can perform at home with a trimmer especially designed for use with dogs. I prefer those with plier grips. They're easier to handle and quite cost effective, selling for under $20 / £11.88.

Snip off the nail tips at a 45-degree angle, being careful not to cut too far down. If you do, you'll catch the vascular quick, which will hurt the dog and cause heavy bleeding. If you are apprehensive about performing this chore, ask your vet tech or groomer to walk you through it the first time.

Anal Glands

All dogs can suffer from blocked anal glands. The dog may scoot or rub its bottom on the ground or carpet. (You may also notice a foul odor.) If this occurs, the glands will need expressing to prevent an abscess from forming. This is a sensitive task and one that a veterinarian or an experienced groomer should perform.

Fleas And Ticks

I'm including fleas and ticks under grooming because that's when they're usually found. Don't think that if your Labradoodle has "passengers," you're doing something wrong or that the dog is at fault. This is a part of dog ownership. Sooner or later, it will happen. Address the problem, but don't "freak out."

Do NOT use a commercial flea product on a puppy of less than 12 weeks of age, and be extremely careful with adult dogs. Most of the major products contain pyrethrum. This chemical causes long-term neurological damage and even fatalities in small dogs.

To get rid of fleas, bathe your dog in warm water with a standard canine shampoo. Comb the animal's fur with a fine-toothed flea comb, which will trap the live parasites. Submerge the comb in hot soapy water to kill the fleas.

Wash the dog's bedding and any soft materials with which he has come in contact. Look for any accumulations of "flea dirt," which is blood excreted by adult fleas. Wash the bedding and other surfaces daily for at least a week to kill any remaining eggs before they hatch.

If you find a tick, coat it with a thick layer of petroleum jelly for 5 minutes to suffocate the parasite and cause its jaws to release. Pluck the tick off with a pair of tweezers using a straight motion. Never just jerk a tick off a dog. The parasite's head stays behind and continues to burrow into the skin, making a painful sore.

Collar or Harness?

Regardless of breed, I'm not a big fan of using a traditional collar. I wouldn't enjoy a choking sensation and assume my dog wouldn't either. My current favorite on-body restraints are the harnesses that look like vests. They offer a point of attachment for the lead on the back between the shoulders.

This arrangement directs pressure away from the neck and allows for easy, free movement. Young dogs are less resistant to this system and don't strain against a harness the way they will with a collar.

It's best to take your dog with you to the pet store to get a proper fit. Sizing for a dog is much more unpredictable than you might think. I have seen dogs as large as 14 lbs. / 6.35 kg take an "Extra Small," depending on their build.

Regardless of size, harnesses retail in a range of $20 - $25 / £11.88 - £14.85

Standard Leash or Retractable?

The decision to buy a standard, fixed-length leash or a retractable lead is, for the most part, a matter of personal preference. Some facilities like groomers, vet clinics and dog daycares ask that you not use a retractable lead on their premises. The long line represents a trip and fall hazard for other human clients.

Fixed length leashes often sell for as little as $5 / £2.97, while retractable leads are less than $15 / £8.91.

Learning to respond to your control of the leash is an important behavioral lesson for your Labradoodle. Do not drag a dog on a lead or jerk him. If your pet sits down and refuses to budge, pick him up. Don't let the dog be in charge of the walk, or you'll have the devil's own time regaining the upper hand.

Labradoodles are smart, active dogs. They'll associate the lead with adventures and time with you. Don't be at all surprised if your dog picks up words associated with excursions like go, out, car, drive or walk.

Photo Credit: Barb Gaffney of Gemstone Labradoodles

Dog Walking Tips

Labradoodles are loving dogs by day and cuddling, snoring companions in the evening. With proper training and adequate exercise, they are well-behaved, delightful pets.

Active dogs like Labradoodles are "into" the whole walking experience. This is an excellent opportunity to use the activity to build and reinforce good behaviors on command.

Teach your dog to "sit" by using the word and making a downward pointing motion with your finger or the palm of your hand. Do not attach the lead until your dog complies, rewarding his patience with the words he most wants to hear: "Okay, let's go!"

If your dog jerks or pulls on the leash, stop, pick up the dog and start the walk over with the "sit" command. Make it clear that the walk ceases when the dog misbehaves.

Praise your dog for walking well on the end of the lead and for stopping when you stop. Reinforce positive behaviors during walks. Your dog will get the message and show the same traits during other activities.

The Importance of Basic Commands

It is to your advantage to go through a basic obedience class with your dog. By their nature, canines are eager to please, but they need direction. Much of this lies in a consistent routine and command "language."

Experts agree that most dogs can pick up between 165 and 200 words, but they can't extrapolate more than one meaning. If, for instance, your dog barks, you need to use the same "command" in response, like "quiet."

If he picks something up, you might say "drop it." For problem jumping, most owners go with "down." The point is to pick a set of words and use them over and over again to create a basic vocabulary for your dog. Both the word and your tone of voice should convey your authority and elicit the desired response.

This is not a difficult process with a breed whose native intelligence is as advanced as that of the Labradoodle. Investigate enrollment in on obedience class through your local big box pet store, or ask your vet about trainers in your area. Start the lessons early in your dog's life by offering him the stability of consistent reactions.

Play Time and Tricks

Labradoodles have a reputation for being trainable dogs. They immediately understand when shown how to shake hands or roll over. They may even add their own creative twist and look at you like, "Do you get it?" Cater to some natural tendency for the first trick and then extrapolate.

Always offer praise and show pleasure for correct responses. This makes training just another form of play – and Labradoodles love to play. The speed with which your dog will amass and destroy a collection of toys may shock you.

Play time is important, especially for a dog's natural desire to chase. Try channeling this instinct with toys and games. If a dog has no stimulation and has nothing to chase, they can start to chase their own tail, which can lead to problems.

Toys can be used to simulate the dog's natural desire to hunt. For example, when they catch a toy they will often shake it and bury their teeth into it, simulating the killing of their prey.

Allow your dog to fulfill a natural desire to chew. This comes from historically catching their prey and then chewing the carcass. Providing chews or bones can prevent your dog from destroying your home.

Playing with your dog is not only a great way of getting them to use up their energy, but it is also a great way of bonding with them as they have fun. Dogs love to chase and catch balls, just make sure that the ball is too large to be swallowed.

Deer antlers are wonderful toys for Labradoodles. Most love them. They do not smell, are all-natural and do not stain or splinter. I recommend the antlers that are not split, as the split ones do not last as long.

Photo Credit: Tracy A. Wynn of Desert Winds Labradoodles

Don't select toys that are soft and "shred-able." I recommend chew toys like Nylabones that can withstand the abuse. You can buy items made out of this tough material in the $1-$5 / £0.59-£2.97 range.

Never give your dog rawhide or pig's ears, which soften and present a choking hazard. Also avoid cow hooves, which can splinter and puncture the cheek or palate.

Avoid soft rubber toys. They shred into small pieces, which the dog will swallow. Opt for rope toys instead. Don't buy anything that presents a choking hazard.

Chapter 6 - Training and Problem Behaviors

Labradoodles are agreeable, good-natured dogs. They have a reputation for being gentle and excellent with small children. Still, any dog can exhibit poor behaviors. Some animals are high strung. Others can be possessive about their territory and human companions. These are all Poodle traits that may surface in the Labradoodle mix.

Negative behavior may not target humans. The dog may act out toward other dogs through snapping, lunging, pushing, barking or baring of the teeth. Most of these potential problem behaviors can be overcome with proper socialization that starts at a young age.

Take your puppy to a training class. Introduce him to new sights, sounds, people and places. Let him interact with other dogs in a controlled environment. There, the dog is safe to deal with fear and timidity without blustering self-defense postures.

You'll get a better-mannered dog and a greater understanding of how to guide your pet's future interactions.

Responsible dog owners are attentive to the behavior of their own dog and what's going on around them. They praise good behavior, but accept responsibility for anticipating potential clashes. Often in a public setting, the wisest course of action is to avoid a meeting with another dog altogether.

In the last chapter, I discussed leash training, which is crucial for successful public outings. Rather than avoiding areas with other people and dogs, your goal is to be able to take your dog to such places without incident.

Labradoodles thrive on interaction and will be happily engaged in interesting public places like parks, walking trails or beaches that are full of new sights, sounds and smells. Contrary to what some people think, well-managed outings in varied environments help to create confidence in your dog.

Dog Whispering

Many people can be confused when they need professional help with their dog because for many years, if you needed help with your dog, you contacted a "dog trainer" or took your dog to "puppy classes" where your dog would learn how to sit or stay.

The difference between a dog trainer and a dog whisperer would be that a "dog trainer" teaches a dog how to perform certain tasks, and a "dog whisperer" alleviates behavior problems by teaching humans what they need to do to keep their particular dog happy.

Often, depending on how soon the guardian has sought help, this can mean that the dog in question has developed some pretty serious issues, such as aggressive barking, lunging, biting or attacking other dogs, pets or people.

Dog whispering is often an emotional roller coaster ride for the humans involved that unveils many truths when they finally realize that it has been their actions (or inactions) that have likely caused the unbalanced behavior that their dog is now displaying.

Once solutions are provided, the relief for both dog and human can be quite cathartic when they realize that with the correct direction, they can indeed live a happy life with their dog.

All specific methods of training, such as "clicker training," fall outside of what every dog needs to be happy, because training your dog to respond to a clicker, which you can easily do on your own, and then letting them sleep in your bed, eat from your plate and any other multitude of things humans allow, are what makes the dog unbalanced and causes behavior problems.

I always say to people, don't wait until you have a severe problem before getting some dog whispering or professional help of some sort, because "With the proper training, Man can learn to be dog's best friend."

Rewarding Unwanted Behavior

It is very important to recognize that any attention paid to an out-of-control, adolescent puppy, even negative attention, is likely to be exciting and rewarding for your Labradoodle puppy.

Chasing after a puppy when they have taken something they shouldn't have, picking them up when barking or showing aggression, pushing them off when they jump on other people, or yelling when they refuse to come when called are all forms of attention that can actually be rewarding for most puppies.

It will be your responsibility to provide structure for your puppy, which will include finding acceptable and safe ways to allow your puppy to vent their energy without being destructive or harmful to others.

The worst thing you can do when training your Labradoodle is to yell at him or use punishment. Positive reinforcement training methods – that is, rewarding your dog for good behavior – are infinitely more effective than negative reinforcement – training by punishment.

It is important when training your Labradoodle that you do not allow yourself to get frustrated. If you feel yourself starting to get angry, take a break and come back to the training session later.

Why is punishment-based training so bad? Think about it this way – your dog should listen to you because he wants to please you, right?

If you train your dog using punishment, he could become fearful of you, and that could put a damper on your relationship with him. Do your dog and yourself a favor by using positive reinforcement.

Teaching Basic Commands

When it comes to training your Labradoodle, you have to start off slowly with the basic commands. The most popular basic commands for dogs include sit, down, stay and come.

Sit

This is the most basic and one of the most important commands you can teach your Labradoodle.

1.) Stand in front of your Labradoodle with a few small treats in your pocket.

2.) Hold one treat in your dominant hand and wave it in front of your Labradoodle's nose so he gets the scent.

3.) Give the "Sit" command.

4.) Move the treat upward and backward over your Labradoodle's head so he is forced to raise his head to follow it.

5.) In the process, his bottom will lower to the ground.

6.) As soon as your Labradoodle's bottom hits the ground, praise him and give him the treat.

7.) Repeat this process several times until your dog gets the hang of it and responds consistently.

Down

After the "Sit" command, "Down" is the next logical command to teach because it is a progression from "Sit."

1.)   Kneel in front of your Labradoodle with a few small treats in your pocket.

2.)   Hold one treat in your dominant hand and give your Labradoodle the "Sit" command.

3.)   Reward your Labradoodle for sitting, then give him the "Down" command.

4.)   Quickly move the treat down to the floor between your Labradoodle's paws.

5.)   Your dog will follow the treat and should lie down to retrieve it.

6.)   Praise and reward your Labradoodle when he lies down.

7.)   Repeat this process several times until your dog gets the hang of it and responds consistently.

Come

It is very important that your Labradoodle responds to a "Come" command, because there may come a time when you need to get his attention and call him to your side during a dangerous situation (such as him running around too close to traffic).

1.)   Put your Labradoodle on a short leash and stand in front of him.

2.)   Give your Labradoodle the "Come" command, then quickly take a few steps backward away from him.

3.)   Clap your hands and act excited, but do not repeat the "Come" command.

4.)   Keep moving backwards in small steps until your Labradoodle follows and comes to you.

5.)   Praise and reward your Labradoodle and repeat the process.

6.)   Over time, you can use a longer leash or take your Labradoodle off the leash entirely.

7.)   You can also start by standing further from your Labradoodle when you give the "Come" command.

8.)   If your Labradoodle doesn't come to you immediately, you can use the leash to pull him toward you.

Stay

This command is very important because it teaches your Labradoodle discipline – not only does it teach your Labradoodle to stay, but it also forces him to listen/pay attention to you.

1.)   Find a friend to help you with this training session.

2.)   Have your friend hold your Labradoodle on the leash while you stand in front of the dog.

3.)   Give your Labradoodle the "Sit" command and reward him for responding correctly.

4.)   Give your dog the "Stay" command while holding your hand out like a "Stop" sign.

5.)   Take a few steps backward away from your dog and pause for 1 to 2 seconds.

6.)   Step back toward your Labradoodle, then praise and reward your dog.

7.)   Repeat the process several times, then start moving back a little further before you return to your dog.

Beyond Basic Training

Once your Labradoodle has a firm grasp on the basics, you can move on to teaching him additional commands. You can also add distractions to the equation to reinforce your dog's mastery of the commands. The end goal is to ensure that your Labradoodle responds to your command each and every time – regardless of distractions and anything else he might rather be doing. This is incredibly important because there may come a time when your dog is in a dangerous situation and if he doesn't respond to your command, he could get hurt.

After your Labradoodle has started to respond correctly to the basic commands on a regular basis, you can start to incorporate distractions.

If you previously conducted your training sessions indoors, you might consider moving them outside where your dog could be distracted by various sights, smells and sounds.

One thing you might try is to give your dog the Stay command, and then toss a toy nearby that will tempt him to break his Stay. Start by tossing the toy at a good distance from him and wait a few seconds before you release him to play.

Eventually you will be able to toss a toy right next to your dog without him breaking his Stay until you give him permission to do so.

Incorporating Hand Signals

Teaching your Labradoodle to respond to hand signals in addition to verbal commands is very useful – you never know when you will be in a situation where your dog might not be able to hear you.

To start out, choose your dominant hand to give the hand signals and hold a small treat in that hand while you are training your dog – this will encourage your dog to focus on your hand during training, and it will help to cement the connection between the command and the hand signal.

To begin, give your dog the Sit or Down command while holding the treat in your dominant hand and give the appropriate hand signal – for Sit you might try a closed fist and, for Down, you might place your hand flat, parallel to the ground.

When your dog responds correctly, give him the treat. You will need to repeat this process many times in order for your dog to form a connection between both the verbal command and the hand signal with the desired behavior.

Eventually, you can start to remove the verbal command from the equation – use the hand gesture every time, but start to use the verbal command only half the time.

Once your dog gets the hang of this, you should start to remove the food reward from the equation. Continue to give your dog the hand signal for each command and occasionally use the verbal command just to remind him.

You should start to phase out the food rewards, however, by offering them only half the time. Progressively lessen the use of the food reward, but continue to praise your dog for performing the behavior correctly so he learns to repeat it.

Teaching Distance Commands

In addition to getting your dog to respond to hand signals, it is also useful to teach him to respond to your commands even when you are not directly next to him.

This may come in handy if your dog is running around outside and gets too close to the street – you should be able to give him a Sit or Down command so he stops before he gets into a dangerous situation.

Teaching your dog distance commands is not difficult, but it does require some time and patience.

To start, give your Labradoodle a brief refresher course of the basic commands while you are standing or kneeling right next to him.

Next, give your dog the Sit and Stay commands, then move a few feet away before you give the Come command.

Repeat this process, increasing the distance between you and your dog before giving him the Come command. Be sure to praise and reward your dog for responding appropriately when he does so.

Once your dog gets the hang of coming on command from a distance, you can start to incorporate other commands.

One method of doing so is to teach your dog to sit when you grab his collar. To do so, let your dog wander freely and every once in a while, walk up and grab his collar while giving the Sit command.

After a few repetitions, your dog should begin to respond with a Sit when you grab his collar, even if you do not give the command.

Gradually, you can increase the distance from which you come to grab his collar and give him the command.

After your dog starts to respond consistently when you come from a distance to grab his collar, you can start giving the Sit command without moving toward him.

It may take your dog a few times to get the hang of it, so be patient. If your dog doesn't sit right away, calmly walk up to him and repeat the Sit command, but do not grab his collar this time.

Eventually, your dog will get the hang of it, and you can start to practice using other commands like Down and Stay from a distance.

Photo Credit: Jessica & Nelson Guthrie of Labradoodle Story Tails

Clicker Training

When it comes to training your Labradoodle, you are going to be most successful if you maintain consistency. Labradoodles have a tendency to be a little stubborn, so unless you are very clear with your dog about what your expectations are, he may simply decide not to follow your commands.

A simple way to achieve consistency in training your Labradoodle is to use the principles of clicker training. Clicker training involves using a small handheld device that makes a clicking noise when you press it between your fingers.

Clicker training is based on the theory of operant conditioning, which helps your dog to make the connection between the desired behavior and the offering of a reward.

Labradoodles have a natural desire to please, so if they learn that a certain behavior earns your approval, they will be eager to repeat it – clicker training is a great way to help your dog quickly identify the particular behavior you want him to repeat.

All you have to do is give your Labradoodle a command and, as soon as he performs the behavior, you use the clicker. After you use the clicker, give your dog the reward as you would with any form of positive reinforcement training.

Some of the benefits of clicker training include:

• Very easy to implement – all you need is the clicker.

• Helps your dog form a connection between the command and the desired behavior more quickly.

• You only need to use the clicker until your dog makes the connection, then you can stop.

• May help to keep your dog's attention more effectively if he hears the noise.

Clicker training is just one method of positive reinforcement training that you can consider for training your Labradoodle.

No matter what method you choose, it is important that you maintain consistency and always praise and reward your dog for responding to your commands correctly so he learns to repeat the behavior.

First Tricks

When teaching your Labradoodle their first tricks, in order to give them extra incentive, find a small treat that they would do anything to get, and give the treat as a reward to help solidify a good performance.

Most dogs will be extra attentive during training sessions when they know that they will be rewarded with their favorite treats. If your Labradoodle is less than six months old when you begin teaching them tricks, keep your training sessions short (no more than 5 or 10 minutes) and make the sessions lots of fun.

As your Labradoodle becomes an adult, you can extend your sessions because they will be able to maintain their focus for longer periods of time.

Shake a Paw

Who doesn't love a dog who knows how to shake a paw? This is one of the easiest tricks to teach your Labradoodle.

Practice every day until they are 100% reliable with this trick, and then it will be time to add another trick to their repertoire.

Most dogs are naturally either right or left pawed. If you know which paw your dog favors, ask them to shake this paw.

Find a quiet place to practice, without noisy distractions or other pets, and stand or sit in front of your dog. Place them in the sitting position and hold a treat in your left hand.

Say the command "Shake" while putting your right hand behind their left or right paw and pulling the paw gently toward yourself until you are holding their paw in your hand. Immediately praise them and give them the treat.

Most dogs will learn the "Shake" trick very quickly, and in no time at all, once you put out your hand, your Labradoodle will immediately lift their paw and put it into your hand, without your assistance or any verbal cue.

Roll Over

You will find that just like your Labradoodle is naturally either right or left pawed, that they will also naturally want to roll either to the right or the left side.

Take advantage of this by asking your dog to roll to the side they naturally prefer. Sit with your dog on the floor and put them in a lie down position.

Hold a treat in your hand and place it close to their nose without allowing them to grab it, and while they are in the lying position, move the treat to the right or left side of their head so that they have to roll over to get to it.

You will quickly see which side they want to naturally roll to; once you see this, move the treat to that side. Once they roll over to that side, immediately give them the treat and praise them.

You can say the verbal cue "Over" while you demonstrate the hand signal motion (moving your right hand in a half circular motion) from one side of their head to the other.

Sit Pretty

While this trick is a little more complicated, and most dogs pick up on it very quickly, remember that this trick requires balance, and every dog is different, so always exercise patience.

Find a quiet space with few distractions and sit or stand in front of your dog and ask them to "Sit."

Have a treat nearby (on a countertop or table) and when they sit, use both of your hands to lift up their front paws into the sitting pretty position, while saying the command "Sit Pretty." Help them balance in this position while you praise them and give them the treat.

Once your Labradoodle can do the balancing part of the trick quite easily without your help, sit or stand in front of your dog while asking them to "Sit Pretty" and hold the treat above their head, at the level their nose would be when they sit pretty.

Photo Credit: Brenda Van Deilen of Calypso Breeze Labradoodles

If they attempt to stand on their back legs to get the treat, you may be holding the treat too high, which will encourage them to stand up on their back legs to reach it. Go back to the first step and put them back into the "Sit" position and again lift their paws while their backside remains on the floor.

The hand signal for "Sit Pretty" is a straight arm held over your dog's head with a closed fist. Place your Labradoodle beside a wall when first teaching this trick so that they can use the wall to help their balance.

A young Labradoodle puppy should be able to easily learn these basic tricks before they are six months old, and when you are patient and make your training sessions short and fun for your dog, they will be eager to learn more.

Excessive Jumping

Allowing any dog to jump is a serious mistake. These animals can get completely out of control. They knock things and people over and scratch people in their exuberant enthusiasm. This is one of the most undesirable of all traits in a dog, especially if the animal has muddy paws or is meeting a frail person. Many people are afraid of dogs and find spontaneous jumping threatening.

Don't make the mistake of assuming that excessive jumping is an expression of friendliness. All too often, it's a case of a dominant dog asserting his authority and saying, "I don't respect you." Dogs that know their proper place in the "pack" don't jump on more dominant dogs. A jumper sees himself as the "top dog" in all situations.

As the dog's master, you must enforce the "no jumping" rule. Anything else will only confuse your pet. Dogs have a keen perception of space. Rather than retreating from a jumping dog, step sideways and forward, taking back your space that he is trying to claim.

You are not trying to knock your dog down, but he may careen into you and fall. Remain casual and calm. Take slow, deliberate motions and protect the "bubble" around your body. Your dog won't be expecting this action from you, and won't enjoy it.

After several failed jumps, the dog will lose interest when his dominant message is no longer getting across.

Barking Behavior

Excessive barking creates serious problems, especially if you live near other people. If you are in an apartment complex with shared walls, a barking dog can get you thrown out of your home. To get to the bottom of problem barking, you must first try to figure out what is setting your dog off.

Is he lonely? bored? wanting attention? overly excited? anxious? Is he responding to something he's seeing? hearing? smelling?

As with all problem behaviors, address barking with patience and consistency. If a firm "No" or "Quiet" fails to work, try spraying your dog with water from a mister or squirt gun. Aim for the face. You won't hurt your pet, but you will get his attention. (Do be careful about your pet's eyes.)

For real problem barkers, humane bark collars can teach the dog through negative reinforcement. These collars release a harmless spray of citronella into the dog's nose in response to vibrations in the throat. The system, though somewhat expensive at $100/£60, works in almost all cases.

Chewing

Chewing is a natural behavior in dogs you must direct in positive ways to prevent damage and destruction in the home. Excessive chewing indicates some combination of anxiety or boredom, which may mean you need to get your dog out of the house more.

Regardless, make sure that your dog has proper chew toys like Nylabones that exist to be destroyed! If you catch your pet chewing on a forbidden object, reprimand him and take the item away. Immediately substitute an appropriate chew toy.

Digging

Digging indoors, like barking and chewing, can be an expression of fear, anxiety and/or boredom. Because the breed is also prone to separation anxiety, the Labradoodle may well be trying to dig his way out to come find you.

Digging is a difficult behavior to stop. An out-of-control digger can destroy your sofa or some other piece of furniture. The best solution is to spend more time playing with and exercising your pet. Also, consider enrolling your pet in a dog daycare facility so he will not be alone while you are at work.

Begging

Any dog will beg at the table if allowed to do so. My best advice to you is to never allow this behavior to get started. Make "people" food off limits from day one.

If your pet becomes a serious beggar, confine him to another part of the house during meal times. This is as a control measure for you and other people at the table. If you can't ignore a plaintive, begging set of Labradoodle eyes, you're the real problem!

Chasing

Labradoodles are excellent runners and all too likely to give into their natural instinct to chase things. This can be an enormous danger to your dog if he is not restrained.

When you are out with your dog, especially near busy urban areas, you must keep your pet leashed at all times. Never allow your dog off the leash unless you are in a fenced, completely secure area. Many dogs become so intent on the chase, they will not come when called.

Biting

It is rare for a Labradoodle to exhibit problem biting. Puppies will nip and bite when they play, a behavior that should be gently curbed before it becomes a problem.

Any dog will bite if he is reacting out of pain or fear. Biting is a primary means of defense. Use socialization, obedience training and stern corrections to control a puppy's playful nips.

If an adult dog displays biting behavior, it is imperative to get to the bottom of the biting. Have the dog evaluated for a health problem and work with a professional trainer. Again, this is a rare concern with Labradoodles.

Chapter 7 – Labradoodle Health

You are your Labradoodle's primary healthcare provider. You will know what is "normal" for your dog. Yours will be the best sense that something is "wrong," even when there is no obvious injury or illness. The more you understand preventive healthcare, the better you will care for your dog throughout his life.

Your Veterinarian Is Your Partner

Working with a qualified veterinarian is critical to long-term and comprehensive healthcare. If you do not already have a vet, ask your breeder for a recommendation. If you purchased your pet outside your area, contact your local dog club and ask for referrals.

Make an appointment to tour the clinic and meet the vet. Be clear about the purpose of your visit and about your intent to pay the regular office fee. Don't expect to get a freebie interview and don't waste anyone's time! Go in with a set of prepared questions. Be sure to cover the following points:

- How long has this practice been in operation?
- How many vets are on staff?
- Are any of your doctors specialists?
- If not, to which doctors do you refer patients?
- What are your regular business hours?
- Do you recommend a specific emergency clinic?
- Do you have emergency hours?
- What specific medical services do you offer?
- Do you offer grooming services?
- May I have an estimated schedule of fees?
- Do you currently treat any Labradoodles?

Pay attention to all aspects of your visit, including how the facilities appear, and the demeanor of the staff. Things to look for include:

- how the staff interacts with clients
- the degree of organization or lack thereof
- indications of engagement with the clientele (office bulletin board, cards and photos displayed, etc.)
- quality of all visible equipment
- cleanliness and orderliness of the waiting area and back rooms
- prominent display of doctors' credentials

These are only some suggestions. Go with your "gut." If the clinic and staff seems to "feel" right to you, trust your instincts. If not, no matter how well appointed the practice may appear to be, visit more clinics before making a decision.

First Visit to the Vet

When you are comfortable with a vet practice, schedule a second visit to include your Labradoodle puppy. Bring all the dog's medical records. Be ready to discuss completing vaccinations and having the animal spayed or neutered. Routine exam procedures include temperature and a check of heart and lung function with a stethoscope. The vet will weigh and measure the puppy. These baseline numbers will help chart growth and physical progress. If you have specific questions, prepare them in advance.

Vaccinations

A puppy's recommended vaccinations begin at 6-7 weeks of age. The first injection covers distemper, hepatitis, parvovirus, parainfluenza and coronavirus.

Recommended boosters occur at 9, 12 and 16 weeks. In some geographical regions, a vaccine for Lyme disease starts at 16 weeks with a booster at 18 weeks.

The rabies vaccination is administered at 12-16 weeks and yearly for life thereafter.

Evaluating for Worms

Puppies purchased from a breeder are almost always parasite free. Worms are more common in rescue dogs and strays. Roundworms appear as small white granules around the anus. Other types of worms can only be seen through a microscope.

These tests are important since some parasites, like tapeworms, may be life threatening. Before a puppy's first visit, the vet will ask for a fecal sample for this purpose. If the puppy tests positive, the standard treatment is a deworming agent with a follow-up dose in 10 days.

Spaying and Neutering

Most Labradoodle breeders practice early spay/neuter before the puppy leaves them, OR they require their families to have spay/neuter done by a certain age per their adoption contract.

I recommend you move forward with either procedure. Altering animals eliminates unwanted pregnancies and offers significant associated health benefits.

Neutering reduces the risk of prostatic disease or perianal tumors in male dogs. The surgery lessens aggressive behaviors, territorial instincts, urine marking and inappropriate mounting.

Spayed females have a diminished risk for breast cancer and no prospect of uterine or ovarian cancer. There are no mood swings related to hormones or issues around the dog coming into season.

Photo Credit: Sabrina Alstat of Sabrinas Labradoodles

"Normal" Health Issues

Although Labradoodles are vigorous, healthy dogs, all canines can face medical issues. The following are "normal" health-related matters that may need veterinary evaluation.

Pets that are inattentive or lethargic and that are not eating or drinking should be examined. None of these behaviors are normal for a Labradoodle.

Diarrhea

Labradoodle puppies are subject to digestive upsets. Puppies just will get into things they shouldn't, like human food or even the kitchen garbage. Diarrhea from these causes resolves within 24 hours. During that time, the puppy should have only small portions of dry food and no treats. Give the dog lots of fresh, clean water to guard against dehydration. If the loose, watery stools are still present after 24 hours, take your Labradoodle to the vet.

The same period of watchful waiting applies for adult dogs. If episodic diarrhea becomes chronic, take a good look at your pet's diet. Chances are good the dog is getting too much rich, fatty food and needs less fat and protein. Some dogs also do better eating small amounts of food several times a day rather than having 2-3 larger meals.

Allergy testing can identify the causes of some cases of diarrhea. Many small dogs are allergic to chicken and turkey. A change in diet resolves their gastrointestinal upset immediately. Diets based on rabbit or duck are often used for dogs with such intolerances.

Either a bacteria or a virus can cause diarrhea, which accompanies fever and vomiting. Parasites, in particular tapeworms and roundworms, may also be to blame.

Coccidia or Giardia are two more possible causes of diarrhea, aside from a food or intestinal issue due to eating something that caused a problem. They are common issues and definitely require medication to treat.

Vomiting

Dietary changes or the puppy "getting into something" can also cause vomiting. Again, this should resolve within 24 hours. If the dog tries to vomit but can't bring anything up, vomits blood or can't keep water down, take your pet to the vet immediately.

Dehydration from vomiting occurs faster than in a case of diarrhea, and can be fatal. It is possible that your dog may need intravenous fluids.

When your dog is vomiting, always have a good look around to identify what, if anything, the dog may have chewed and swallowed. This can be a huge benefit in targeting appropriate treatment.

Other potential culprits include: hookworm, roundworm, pancreatitis, diabetes, thyroid disease, kidney disease, liver disease or a physical blockage.

Bloat

Any dog can suffer from bloat, but some are at higher risk than others. Also known as gastric dilation / volvulus or GDV, bloat cannot be treated with an antibiotic or prevented with a vaccine. If left untreated, the condition can be fatal.

In severe cases, the stomach twists partially or completely. This causes circulation problems throughout the digestive system. Dogs that do not receive treatment go into cardiac arrest. Even if surgical intervention is attempted, there is no guarantee of success.

Signs of bloat are often mistaken for indications of excess gas. The dog may salivate and attempt to vomit, pace and whine. Gas reduction products at this stage can be helpful. As the stomach swells, it places pressure on surrounding vital organs and may burst.

All cases of bloat are a *serious* medical emergency.

Risk Factors

Larger dogs with deep chests and small waists face a greater risk of developing bloat. These include the Great Dane, Weimaraner, Saint Bernard, Irish Setter and the Standard Poodle.

Eating habits also factor into the equation. Dogs that eat one large meal per day consisting of dry food are in a high-risk category. Feed three small meals throughout the day. This helps to prevent gulping, which leads to ingesting large amounts of air.

Experts recommend dry food for dogs, but don't let your pet drink lots of water after eating. Doing so causes the dry food in the stomach to expand, leading to discomfort and a dilution of the digestive juices.

Limit the amount of play and exercise after meals. A slow walk promotes digestion, but a vigorous romp can be dangerous.

Stress also contributes to bloat, especially in anxious or nervous dogs. Changes in routine, confrontations with other dogs and moving to a new home can all trigger an attack.

Dogs between the ages of 4 and 7 are at an increased risk. Bloat occurs most often between 2 a.m. and 6 a.m., roughly 10 hours after the animal has had his dinner.

Prevention

Feed your pet small meals 2-3 times a day, limiting both water intake and exercise after eating. Take up your pet's water at mealtime and do not offer it to the dog for at least 30 minutes after your pet finishes his meal. Do not allow strenuous activity for at least an hour.

Test your dog's dry food by putting a serving in a bowl with water. Leave the material to expand overnight. If the degree of added bulk seems excessive, consider switching to a premium or organic food.

Keep an anti-gas medicine with simethicone on hand. (Consult with your veterinarian on correct dosage.) Consider adding a probiotic to your dog's food to reduce gas in the stomach and to improve digestive health.

If a dog experiences bloat once, his risk of a future episode is greater. Keep copies of his medical records at home and know the location of the nearest emergency vet clinic.

Allergies

Like humans, dogs suffer from allergies. Food, airborne particles and materials that touch the skin can all cause reactions. Owners tend to notice changes in behavior that suggest discomfort like itching. Common symptoms include chewing or biting of the tail, stomach or hind legs, or licking of the paws.

In reaction to inhaled substances, the dog will sneeze, cough or experience watering eyes. Ingested substances may lead to vomiting or diarrhea. Dogs can also suffer from rashes or a case of hives. Your poor Labradoodle can be just as miserable as you are during an allergy attack.

If the reaction occurs in the spring or fall, the likely culprit is seasonal pollen or, in the case of hot weather, fleas. Food additives like beef, corn, wheat, soybeans and dairy products can all cause gastrointestinal upset.

As with any allergy, take away suspect items or try a special diet. Allergy testing offers a definitive diagnosis and pinpoints necessary environmental and dietary changes. The tests are expensive, costing $200+ / £120+. The vet may recommend medication or bathing the dog in cool, soothing water. Special diets are also extremely helpful.

For acne-like chin rashes, switch to stainless steel, glass or ceramic food dishes. Plastic feeding dishes cause this rash, which looks like blackheads surrounded by inflamed skin. Wash the dog's face in clear, cool water and ask the vet for an antibiotic cream to speed the healing process.

General Signs of Illness

Any of the following symptoms can point to a serious medical problem. Have your pet evaluated for any of these behaviors. Don't wait out of fear that you are just being an alarmist. Vets can resolve most medical problems in dogs if treatment starts at the first sign of illness.

Coughing and/or Wheezing

Occasional coughing is not a cause for concern, but if it goes on for more than a week, a vet visit is in order. A cough may indicate:

- kennel cough
- heartworm
- cardiac disease
- bacterial infections
- parasites
- tumors
- or allergies

The upper respiratory condition called "kennel cough" presents with a dry, hacking cough. It is a form of canine bronchitis caused by warm, overcrowded conditions with poor ventilation. In most cases, kennel cough resolves on its own.

Consult with your veterinarian. The doctor may prescribe a cough suppressant or suggest the use of a humidifier to soothe your pet's irritated airways.

When the cause of a cough is unclear, the vet will take a full medical history and order tests, including blood work and X-rays. Fluid may also be drawn from the lungs for analysis. Among other conditions, the doctor will be attempting to rule out heartworms.

A Note on Heartworms

Mosquitos spread heartworms (*Dirofilaria Immitis*) through their bites. They are thin, long parasites that infest the muscles of the heart, where they block blood vessels and cause bleeding. Their presence can lead to heart failure and death. Coughing and fainting, as well as an intolerance to exercise, are all symptoms of heartworm. Discuss heartworm prevention with your vet and decide on the best course of action to keep your pet safe.

Other Warning Signs

Additional warning signs include:

- excessive and unexplained drooling
- excessive consumption of water and increased urination
- changes in appetite leading to weight gain or loss

- marked change in levels of activity
- disinterest in favorite activities
- stiffness and difficulty standing or climbing stairs
- sleeping more than normal
- shaking of the head
- any sores, lumps or growths
- dry, red or cloudy eyes

Often the signs of serious illness are subtle. Trust your instincts. If you think something is wrong, do not hesitate to consult with your vet.

Photo Credit: Babbie R. Holden of Royal Diamond Labradoodles

Diabetes

Canines can suffer from three types of diabetes: insipidus, diabetes mellitus and gestational diabetes. All point to malfunctioning endocrine glands and are often linked to poor diet. Larger dogs are in a higher risk category.

- In cases of *diabetes insipidus,* low levels of the hormone vasopressin create problems with the regulation of blood glucose, salt and water.

- Diabetes mellitus is more common and dangerous. It is divided into Types I and II. The first develops in young dogs and may be referred to as "juvenile." Type II is more prevalent in adult and older dogs. All cases are treated with insulin.

- Gestational diabetes occurs in pregnant female dogs and requires the same treatment as diabetes mellitus. Obese dogs are at greater risk.

Abnormal insulin levels interfere with blood sugar levels. Poodles face a high risk for diabetes, a predisposition that can be passed into Labradoodles. In general, though, crossbred dogs have shown more resistance to the condition.

Symptoms of Canine Diabetes

All of the following behaviors are signs that a dog is suffering from canine diabetes:

- excessive water consumption
- excessive and frequent urination
- lethargy / uncharacteristic laziness
- weight gain or loss for no reason

It is possible your pet may display no symptoms whatsoever. Diabetes can be slow to develop, so the effects may not be immediately noticeable. Regular check-ups help to catch this disease, which can be fatal even when you do not realize that anything is wrong.

Managing Diabetes

As part of a diabetes management program, the vet will recommend diet changes, including special food. Your dog may need insulin injections. Although this may sound daunting, your vet will train you to administer the shots. A dog with diabetes can live a full and normal life. Expect regular visits to the vet to check for heart and circulatory problems.

Dental Care

Chewing is a dog's only means of maintaining his teeth. Many of our canine friends develop dental problems early in life because they don't get enough of this activity. Not all dogs are prone to cavities. Most do suffer from accumulations of plaque and associated gum diseases. Often, severe halitosis (bad breath) is the first sign that something is wrong.

With dental problems, gingivitis develops first and, if unaddressed, progresses to periodontitis. Warning signs of gum disease include:

- a reluctance to finish meals
- extreme bad breath
- swollen and bleeding gums
- irregular gum line
- plaque build-up
- drooling and/or loose teeth

The smaller Poodle varieties are prone to gingivitis, which places Labradoodles at a higher risk as well.

The bacterial gum infection periodontitis causes inflammation, gum recession and possible tooth loss. It requires treatment with antibiotics to prevent a spread of the infection to other parts of the body. Symptoms include:

- pus at the gum line
- loss of appetite
- depression
- irritability
- pawing at the mouth
- trouble chewing
- loose or missing teeth
- gastrointestinal upset

Treatment begins with a professional cleaning. This procedure may also involve root work, descaling and even extractions.

With Proliferating Gum Disease, the gums overgrow the teeth, causing inflammation and infection. Symptoms include:

- thickening and lengthening of the gums
- bleeding
- bad breath
- drooling
- loss of appetite

The vet will prescribe antibiotics, and surgery is usually required.

Home Dental Care

There are many products available to help with home dental care for your Labradoodle. Some owners opt for water additives that break up tarter and plaque, but in some cases dogs experience stomach upset. Dental sprays and wipes are also an option, but so is gentle gum massage to help break up plaque and tarter.

Most owners incorporate some type of dental chew in their standard care practices. Greenies Dental Chews for Dogs are popular and well tolerated in a digestive sense. An added plus is that dogs usually love them. The treats come in different sizes and are priced in a range of $7 / £4.21 for 22 "Teeny" Greenies and $25 / £15 for 17 Large Greenies.

Brushing your pet's teeth is the ultimate defense for oral health. This involves the use of both a canine-specific toothbrush and toothpaste. Never use human toothpaste, which contains fluoride toxic to your dog. Some dog toothbrushes resemble smaller versions of our own, but I like the models that just fit over your fingertip. I think they offer greater control and stability.

The real trick to brushing your pet's teeth is getting the dog comfortable with having your hands in his mouth. Start by just massaging the dog's face, and then progressing to the gums before using the toothbrush. In the beginning, you can even just smear the toothpaste on the teeth with your fingertip.

Try to schedule these brushing sessions for when the dog is a little tired, perhaps after a long walk. Don't apply pressure, which can stress the dog. Just move in small circular motions and stop when the Labradoodle has had enough of the whole business. If you don't feel you've done enough, stop. A second session is better than forcing your dog to do something he doesn't like and creating a negative association in his mind.

Even if you do practice a full home dental care routine, don't scrimp on annual oral exams in the vet's office. Exams not only help to keep the teeth and gums healthy, but also to check for the presence of possible cancerous growths.

The Matter of Genetic Abnormalities

The Labradoodle gene pool does contain known genetic diseases. Labrador Retrievers develop hip and elbow dysplasia. They can suffer from eye problems including progressive renal atrophy, cataracts and retinal dysplasia.

Poodles are susceptible to hip dysplasia, progressive renal atrophy and Von Willebrand's disease. The bleeding disorder Von Willebrand's is comparable to hemophilia in humans. It is an incurable condition that prevents proper blood clotting.

Any of these conditions can affect Labradoodles, and not all are identifiable in puppies. For this reason, you are well advised to ask about health testing of the parents and the puppies used to create the cross.

Don't buy a Labradoodle or Australian Labradoodle without proof that these tests have occurred. You should receive a record of shots given and an explanation of the health guarantee. Other tests may include CERF/ACVO* eye exams and those for Brucella Canis**.

* Canine Eye Registration Foundation / American College of Veterinary Opthalmologists

** The gram-negative proteobacterium Brucella Canis causes brucellosis in dogs and other canids.

Rare conditions in Labradoodles include the endocrine disorder Addison's Disease and Sebaceous Adenitis, a malfunction of the skin's oil-producing glands.

As Labradoodles move toward full breed acceptance, health testing will become more standardized. If you are dealing with a casual breeder, advanced health screenings are rare. An owner with an organized breeding program should be able to discuss the topic with you at length. Beware of breeders claiming such tests are unnecessary or who say none of their dogs have ever had a genetic condition.

Luxating Patella

A dog with a luxating patella experiences frequent dislocations of the kneecap. The condition is common in small and miniature breeds, and can affect one or both kneecaps.

Surgery may be required to rectify the problem. Often, owners have no idea anything is wrong with their dog's knee joint. Then the pet jumps off a bed or leaps to catch a toy, lands badly and begins to limp and favor the leg.

The condition may be genetic in origin, so it is important to ask a breeder if the problem has surfaced in the line of dogs he cultivates. A luxating patella can also be the consequence of a physical injury, especially as a dog ages. For this reason, you may want to discourage jumping in older dogs. Offer steps in key locations around the home to help your senior Labradoodle navigate in safety.

Any time you see your dog limping or seeming more fatigued than usual after vigorous play, have the dog checked out. Conditions like a luxating patella only get worse with time and wear, and need immediate treatment.

Hip Dysplasia

Labradoodles may also be susceptible to hip dysplasia. This defect prevents the thighbone from fitting into the hip joint. It is a painful condition that causes limping in the hindquarters. This may be inherited or the consequence of injury and aging.

When hip dysplasia presents, the standard treatment is anti-inflammatory medication. Some cases need surgery and even a full hip replacement. Surgical intervention for this defect carries a high success rate, allowing your dog to live a full and happy life.

Canine Arthritis

Dogs, like humans, can suffer from arthritis. This debilitating degeneration of the joints often affects larger breeds. As the cartilage in the joints breaks down, the action of bone rubbing on bone creates considerable pain. In turn, the animal's range of motion becomes restricted.

Standard treatments do not differ from those used for humans. Aspirin addresses pain and inflammation, while supplements like glucosamine work on improving joint health. Environmental aids, like steps and ramps, ease the strain on the affected joints and help pets stay active.

Arthritis is a natural consequence of aging. Management focuses on making your pet comfortable and facilitating ease of motion. Some dogs become so crippled that their humans buy mobility carts (often also called dog wheelchairs) for them. These devices, which attach to the hips, put your pooch on wheels. Labradoodles adapt well under such circumstances. So long as your pet is otherwise healthy, this is a reasonable approach to a debilitating, but not fatal ailment.

Although the carts are adjustable, having your dog custom fitted for the appliance may provide more mobility.

Photo Credit: Dixie Springer of Springville Labradoodles

Canine Eye Care

Check your dog's eyes on a regular schedule to avoid problems like clogged tear ducts. Also, many dogs suffer from excessive tearing, which can stain the fur around the eyes and down the muzzle. This is a problem with Poodles and can occur in Labradoodles with lighter coats.

As a part of good grooming, keep the corners of your pet's eyes and the muzzle free of mucus to prevent bacterial growth.

If your dog is prone to mucus accumulation, ask your vet for a sterile eyewash or gauze pads. Also consider having the dog tested for environmental allergies.

Take the precaution of keeping the hair well-trimmed around your pet's eyes. If you do not feel comfortable doing this chore yourself, discuss the problem with your groomer. Shorter hair prevents the transference of bacteria and avoids trauma from scrapes and scratches.

Dogs love to hang their heads out of car windows, but this can result in eye injuries and serious infection from blowing debris. If you don't want to deprive your dog of this simple pleasure, I recommend a product called Doggles.

These protective goggles for dogs come in a range of colors and sizes for less than $20 / £12 per pair. The investment in protecting your dog's eyes is well worth it. All my pets have worn the Doggles without complaint.

Conjunctivitis is the most common eye infection seen in dogs. It presents with redness around the eyes and a green or yellow discharge. Antibiotics will treat the infection. The dreaded "cone of shame" collar then prevents more injury from scratching during healing.

Cataracts

Aging dogs often develop cataracts, which is a clouding of the lens of the eye leading to blurred vision. The lesion can vary in size and will be visible as a blue gray area. In most cases, the vet will watch but not treat cataracts. The condition does not affect your pet's life in a severe way. Dogs adapt well to the senses they do have, so diminished vision is not as problematic as it would be for us.

Cherry Eye

The condition called "cherry eye" is an irritation of the third eyelid. It appears as a bright pink protrusion in the corner of the eye. Either injury or a bacterial infection causes cherry eye. It may occur in one or both eyes and requires surgery to effect a permanent cure.

Glaucoma

With glaucoma, increased pressure prevents proper drainage of fluid. Glaucoma may develop on its own or as a complication of a shifted cataract. Dogs with glaucoma experience partial or total loss of vision within one year of diagnosis.

Symptoms include swelling, excessive tearing, redness and evident visual limitations. Suspected glaucoma requires immediate medical attention.

PRA or Progressive Retinal Atrophy

Progressive Retinal Atrophy (PRA), a degenerative hereditary disease, presents with a slow progression. The dog will go blind over time, but most adapt to what is happening to them. Early detection allows for better environmental adaptations. There is no way to prevent or cure PRA. If you suspect your Labradoodle has poor peripheral vision, or if the dog is tentative in low light, have your pet's eyes checked.

Hemorrhagic Gastroenteritis

Any dog can develop hemorrhagic gastroenteritis (HGE). The condition has a high mortality rate. Unfortunately, most dog owners have never heard of HGE. If a dog does not receive immediate treatment, the animal may well die.

Symptoms include:

- profuse vomiting
- depression
- bloody diarrhea with a foul odor
- severe low blood volume resulting in fatal shock within 24 hours

The exact cause of HGE is unknown, and it often occurs in otherwise healthy dogs. The average age of onset is 2-4 years. Approximately 15% of dogs that survive an attack will suffer a relapse. There is no definitive list of high-risk breeds. Those with a high incidence rate include:

- Miniature Poodles
- Miniature Schnauzers
- Yorkshire Terriers
- Dachshunds

The instant your dog vomits or passes blood, get your dog to the vet. Tests will rule out viral or bacterial infections, ulcers, parasites, cancer and poisoning. X-rays and an electrocardiogram are also primary diagnostic tools for HGE.

Hospitalization and aggressive treatment are necessary. The dog will likely need IV fluids and even a blood transfusion. Both steroids and antibiotics prevent infection. If the dog survives, the animal should eat a bland diet for a week or more, with only a gradual reintroduction of normal foods. In almost all cases, the dog will eat a special diet for life with the use of a probiotic.

The acute phases of HGE lasts 2-3 days. With quick and aggressive treatment, many dogs recover well. Delayed intervention for any reason means the outlook is not good.

Tail Docking or Cropping

Breeders use both Labrador Retrievers and Poodles to create the Labradoodle. Neither of those breeds has a short tail. Before the puppy reaches adulthood the tail is "docked" or cut. This is a controversial practice in Labradoodles.

Most owners don't want the dogs to go through painful mutilation for no good reason. Often, the procedure occurs long before puppies come up for adoption. Some breeders take puppies to the vet for the surgery under anesthesia. Others remove the tails within five days of birth.

The assumption is that puppies have underdeveloped nervous systems and don't feel intense pain. Breeders use one of two methods.

- A strong band on the tail cuts off circulation to the tip until it falls off from dry gangrene.

- A clamp on the tail controls bleeding for amputation of the remaining section with a scalpel or scissors.

Regardless of where the procedure occurs, the wound requires stitches.

If you are against docking a dog's tail, make this clear when you contact a breeder. If they know in advance, most will leave the tail intact, but you are then obligated to take the dog.

Docking is illegal in the United Kingdom and Australia. Efforts are underway in parts of the United States to ban the practice, but no laws currently exist.

Photo Credit: Jacqui Carter-Davies of Jacarties Labradoodles

Breeding Labradoodles

Anyone can breed Labradoodles, but the results may be unpredictable. Labradoodles mated with Labrador Retrievers or Poodles often have puppies more like the foundation breeds.

Even Labradoodle to Labradoodle pairings produce unexpected results. Casual pairings have plagued this "hybrid mix" from the beginning. They do no service to the goal of creating a distinct and recognized breed.

Enthusiasts who want the Labradoodle recognized as a breed take on an all-consuming passion. Their goals are different and focused.

They don't buy into the old wives tales about a female dog being healthier for having given birth to a litter before spaying. Real Labradoodle lovers breed only to improve the genetics of the line. They select mated pairs for the likely results in the litter. Meticulous records trace the ancestral bloodline from which further generations will evolve.

This kind of breeding will, in time, overcome inconsistencies and create a stable Labradoodle. The goal is animals that breed "true," passing on predictable qualities. At this stage of the breed's evolution, I recommend against casual backyard matings.

Labradoodles have the potential to be one of the most desirable of all companion breeds. That will only occur if knowledgeable breeders can cultivate and stabilize bloodlines. This is not as simple as allowing your Labrador Retriever to "date" the neighbor's Poodle.

Chapter 8 - Preparing for Older Age

It can be heartbreaking to watch your beloved Labradoodle pet grow older – he may develop health problems like arthritis, and he simply might not be as active as he once was.

Unfortunately, aging is a natural part of life that cannot be avoided. All you can do is learn how to provide for your Labradoodle's needs as he ages, so you can keep him with you for as long as possible.

Photo Credit: Becky & Jim Roth of Southern Cross Australian Labradoodles

What to Expect

Aging is a natural part of life for both humans and dogs. Sadly, dogs reach the end of their lives sooner than most humans do.

Once your Labradoodle reaches the age of 8 years or so, he can be considered a "senior" dog.

At this point, you may need to start feeding him a dog food specially formulated for older dogs, and you may need to take some other precautions as well.

In order to properly care for your Labradoodle as he ages, you might find it helpful to know what to expect. Here is a list of things to expect as your Labradoodle dog starts to get older:

• Your dog may be less active than he was in his youth – he will likely still enjoy walks, but he may not last as long as he once did, and he might take it at a slower pace.

• Your Labradoodle's joints may start to give him trouble – check for signs of swelling and stiffness and consult your veterinarian with any problems.

• Your dog may sleep more than he once did – this is a natural sign of aging, but it can also be a symptom of a health problem, so consult your vet if your dog's sleeping becomes excessive.

• Your dog may have a greater tendency to gain weight, so you will need to carefully monitor his diet to keep him from becoming obese in his old age.

• Your dog may have trouble walking or jumping, so keep an eye on your Labradoodle if he has difficulty jumping or if he starts dragging his back feet.

• Your dog's vision may no longer be as sharp as it once was, so your Labradoodle may be predisposed to these problems.

• You may need to trim your Labradoodle's nails more frequently if he doesn't spend as much time outside as he once did when he was younger.

•   Your dog may be more sensitive to extreme heat and cold, so make sure he has a comfortable place to lie down both inside and outside.

•   Your dog will develop gray hair around the face and muzzle – this may be less noticeable in Labradoodles with a lighter coat.

While many of the signs mentioned above are natural side effects of aging, they can also be symptoms of serious health conditions. If your dog develops any of these problems suddenly, consult your veterinarian immediately.

Caring for an Older Labradoodle

When your Labradoodle gets older, he may require different care than he did when he was younger.

The more you know about what to expect as your Labradoodle ages, the better equipped you will be to provide him with the care he needs to remain healthy and mobile.

Here are some tips for caring for your Labradoodle dog as he ages:

•   Schedule routine annual visits with your veterinarian to make sure your Labradoodle is in good condition.

•   Consider switching to a dog food that is specially formulated for senior dogs – a food that is too high in calories may cause your dog to gain weight.

•   Supplement your dog's diet with DHA and EPA fatty

acids to help prevent joint stiffness and arthritis.

•   Brush your Labradoodle's teeth regularly to prevent periodontal diseases, which are fairly common in older dogs.

•   Continue to exercise your dog on a regular basis – he may not be able to move as quickly, but you still need to keep him active to maintain joint and muscle health.

•   Provide your Labradoodle with soft bedding on which to sleep – the hard floor may aggravate his joints and worsen arthritis.

•   Use ramps to get your dog into the car and onto the bed, if he is allowed, because he may no longer be able to jump.

•   Consider putting down carpet or rugs on hard floors – slippery hardwood or tile flooring can be very problematic for arthritic dogs.

In addition to taking some of the precautions listed above in caring for your elderly Labradoodle, you may want to familiarize yourself with some of the health conditions your dog is likely to develop in his old age.

Elderly dogs are also likely to exhibit certain changes in behavior, including:

- Confusion or disorientation
- Increased irritability
- Decreased responsiveness to commands
- Increase in vocalization (barking, whining, etc.)
- Heightened reaction to sound
- Increased aggression or protectiveness
- Changes in sleep habits

- Increase in house soiling accidents

As your Labradoodle ages, these tendencies may increase – he may also become more protective of you around strangers.

As your Labradoodle gets older, you may find that he responds to your commands even less frequently than he used to.

The most important thing you can do for your senior dog is to schedule regular visits with your veterinarian. You should also, however, keep an eye out for signs of disease as your dog ages.

The following are common signs of disease in elderly dogs:

- Decreased appetite
- Increased thirst and urination
- Difficulty urinating/constipation
- Blood in the urine
- Difficulty breathing/coughing
- Vomiting or diarrhea
- Poor coat condition

If you notice your elderly Labradoodle exhibiting any of these symptoms, you would be wise to seek veterinary care for your dog as soon as possible.

Euthanasia

The hardest decision any pet owner makes is helping a suffering animal to pass easily and humanely. I have been in this position. Even though I know my beloved companions died peacefully and with no pain, my own anguish was considerable. Thankfully, I was in the care of and accepting the advice and counsel of exceptional veterinary professionals.

This is the crucial component in the decision to euthanize an animal. For your own peace of mind, you must know that you have the best medical advice possible. My vet was not only knowledgeable and patient, but she was kind and forthright. I valued those qualities and hope you are as blessed as I was in the same situation.

I am fortunate that I have never been forced to make this decision based on economic necessity. I once witnessed the joy of a biker who sold his beloved motorcycle to pay for cancer treatments for his German Shepherd. The dog meant more to him than the bike, and he burst into tears when the vet said, "We got it all."

But the bottom line is this. No one is in a position to judge you – no one. You must make the best decision that you can for your pet, and for yourself. So long as you are acting from a position of love, respect and responsibility, whatever you do is "right."

Photo Credit: Elizabeth Ferris of Country Labradoodles

Grieving

Many people do not wait long enough before attempting to replace a lost pet and will immediately go to the local shelter and rescue a deserving dog. While this may help to distract you from your grieving process, this is not really fair to the new fur member of your family.

Bringing a new pet into a home that is depressed and grieving the loss of a long-time canine member may create behavioral problems for the new dog that will be faced with learning all about their new home, while also dealing with the unstable energy of the grieving family.

A better scenario would be to allow yourself the time to properly grieve by waiting a minimum of one month to allow yourself and your family to feel happier and more stable before deciding upon sharing your home with another dog.

Managing Health Care Costs

Thanks to advances in veterinary science, our pets now receive viable and effective treatments. The estimated annual cost for a medium-sized dog, including health care, is $650 / £387. (This does not include emergency care, advanced procedures or consultations with specialists.)

The growing interest in pet insurance to help defray these costs is understandable. You can buy a policy covering accidents, illness and hereditary and chronic conditions for $25 / £16.25 per month. Benefit caps and deductibles vary by company.

To obtain rate quotes, investigate the following companies in the United States and the UK:

United States

http://www.24PetWatch.com
http://www.ASPCAPetInsurance.com
http://www.EmbracePetInsurance.com
http://www.HealthyPawsPetInsurance.com
http://www.PetsBest.com
http://www.PetInsurance.com

United Kingdom

http://www.Animalfriends.org.uk
http://www.Petplan.co.uk
http://www.Vetsmedicover.co.uk

Photo Credit: Gayle Husfloen of North Country Australian Labradoodles

Afterword

The Labradoodle's rapid rise in popularity over the past 25 years shows this hybrid's great potential. Merging a Labrador Retriever's good nature with a Poodle's superb intelligence can create a fantastic family dog.

The original plan was to create a hypoallergenic dog, a goal only partially realized in the Labradoodle's current state of evolution. At best, the dogs are better tolerated by allergy sufferers. There is no guarantee that any Labradoodle will have a low-allergy coat.

Most Labradoodles shed little and have no odor. Others, like their Labrador antecedents, leave hair everywhere and carry that trademark "doggy" smell. Such inconsistent results, generally outside organized breeding programs, plague the Labradoodle.

Backyard breeders are testament to the Labradoodle's growing popularity, but they do the breed no service. For-profit-only puppy mills are deplorable on every level. They give no thought to health care, much less genetic integrity.

Thankfully, dedicated enthusiasts continue to work to refine the Labradoodle cross and to seek full acceptance of the breed. I advise that you find a breeder dedicated to cultivating the breed to ensure you get the best dog possible.

When a Labradoodle is "done" right, I know of no dog more loyal, loving and downright fun. There is no other dog quite like them.

Bonus Chapter 1 - Interview With Dana Eckert

Dana, can you tell us who you are and where you are based?

Yes, I am the owner and founder of California Labradoodles. We are based in Northern California.

How long have you been breeding Labradoodles?

We have been breeding for 11 plus years. The idea for California Labradoodles was born in 2002, and we invested a lot of our time and money researching this breed, determining what we wanted our program to look like, and selecting the best possible breeding stock, before we had our first litter in early 2004. Our breeding dogs originated from Australia.

I have three boys, and the idea to breed Australian Labradoodles started with them. My oldest son claims it was his idea, my youngest son says he came up with the idea. I thought it was mine. I honestly don't know who is right. It sort of was like spontaneous combustion. We all loved the idea and embraced it right away, expanding on it as we learned more and more about the breed. At the time I had started a foundation to teach business and entrepreneurship to women in the US and in developing countries. I thought if I could teach business to women, I could teach it to my kids around something we all loved and cherished. We have always been a dog-loving family, and for many, many reasons the idea appealed to all of us. Although it's my youngest son who really helped me with every aspect of raising puppies, and he deserves extra kudos. He helps me deliver pups, clean up after them, socialize them and train them. But we all are involved and it truly is a labor of love.

California Labradoodles was never supposed to be what it became. We initially were going to just create a small family business we could all do together. By the time we imported our first Australian Labradoodle in 2004, we had fallen madly in love with the breed. Pretty soon we had imported another and eventually I dissolved my foundation.

There are a number of variations within the Labradoodle breed, perhaps you could explain which types you breed?

I breed miniature and medium multigeneration Australian Labradoodles. In terms of size, per the Australian Labradoodle breed standard, size is measured by height, not weight. Per the breed standard, a miniature is 14 to 16 inches tall and a medium is 17 to 19 inches tall.

The key difference is between the American Labradoodle (F1) and the Australian Labradoodle – in your opinion how do they differ in practical terms?

In my opinion, the biggest difference between these earlier generation F1 dogs and the Australian Labradoodles I breed is consistency. I get fantastic consistency. I have had incredible success with the allergy friendliness and non-shedding qualities of my dogs. My coats are wonderful. I am breeding for sweetness, calmness and soundness of temperament. My dogs have wonderful, loving temperaments and consistent coats and conformation.

Don't get me wrong, you can get a wonderful early generation American Labradoodle that has it all – looks, coat, temperament etc. I'm just talking about the consistency I get in a litter.

In answer to your question about the key difference between the American Labradoodle and the Australian Labradoodle is where they originated from and the dogs infused into the lines. In practical terms, an F1 Labradoodle is a Lab bred to a Poodle. I breed multigeneration Australian Labradoodles bred to multigeneration Australian Labradoodles. The Australian Labradoodles have been bred for over 30 years and over time have had other breeds infused into the lines to correct certain faults.

Within the Australian Labradoodle, there seems to be a number of different factions and associations, why?

Well that's a harder question to answer. As in any developing breed, there are different personalities and goals amongst breeders. There are some strong personalities in this business as there are in any business. And as in any business, there can be a lot of politics. I think as the breed develops within the US, there are a growing number of breeders, myself included, who want to ensure people breed responsibly. There are more and more people breeding these dogs, and if we are to protect the breed, there needs to be a code of ethics and guidelines and research done to insure we are indeed creating a better dog.

The Australian Labradoodle is still a developing breed. People go into breeding for a lot of different reasons, and have different objectives. Some people think this is a quick way to make money, and trust me it is not. Done correctly, breeding is a very expensive endeavor. We spend a lot of money health testing and caring for our dogs.

Our mission is written on my website and we ask ourselves every day if what we are doing falls within our stated mission.

We do our best to breed responsibly and with integrity. We carefully adhere to the code of ethics and breeding standards of the Australian Labradoodle Association of America (ALAA) and the Australian Labradoodle Club of America (ALCA). We always strive to put the interest of the Australian Labradoodle at the center of everything we do. We stand behind our clients, and offer ongoing support. We love the Australian Labradoodle breed and want to protect these wonderful dogs.

What types of people are buying Labradoodles and why?

I'd say the majority of my clients want an allergy-friendly, family dog with a great temperament. Many, many of my adopting families have allergies and are looking for a dog they can love that won't cause their allergies to flare up. Within that group there is a big range. I have many clients who have children and are looking for a dog that will get along well with their children. I have a lot of retired, elderly clients who want a loving dog that will want to be wherever they are. I have people who are tired of cleaning up the hair that their Labs shed, although they love and adore them. I have clients with special needs, who feel one of our Australian Labradoodles will work well with their particular issue. I have therapists looking for a therapy dog. I have people in dog-friendly work environments looking to bring a dog to work with them. I have several veterinarians who fell in love with the breed after meeting many in their practices. I'd say the majority of my clients want a loving dog to be part of their family, and daily lives.

The Labradoodle is not recognized by the American Kennel Club, is it a question or issue that is raised by many people?

Yes I get that question sometimes, but wouldn't say it is foremost on people's minds. I think what people are more concerned about is the temperament of the dogs we are breeding, and how well they will fit into their families.

What sort of challenges do you face in mating two different breeds?

I breed multigeneration Australian Labradoodle to multigeneration Australian Labradoodle. I have not myself done any infusions.

One challenge we face is getting over the image of the Labradoodle as a designer dog. I really abhor the term "designer dogs." That's not what our dogs are. They are dogs that are bred for a purpose – to be family companion dogs. We are breeding for soundness of temperament. We strive to breed dogs with temperaments that would work well in therapy settings. Not all Australian Labradoodles make good therapy dogs, but that is what we are striving for, and many of them do.

Another challenge is the marketing hype. There is no such thing as a hypoallergenic dog of any breed. That being said our dogs do very well with people with allergies. We've been breeding very consistent, allergy-friendly coats.

What type of health issues can a Labradoodle have and how do you deal with preventing these?

Australian Labradoodles can have any of the health issues found in the original parent breeds. We do as much as we can to screen for inheritable problems. The tests we do include:

Pennhip and OFA to test hips and elbows. We use OFA or CERF to test eyes. CERF is the Canine Eye Registration Foundation and this is a test of the dog's eyes. We do yearly OFA Thyroids and CERF/OFA eyes every 18 months. We also run full CBC panels on our dogs. We screen for PRA. PRA is a disease that causes blindness in older dogs. We look at their hearts, knees, elbows and conformation of the dog. We do several kinds of DNA testing, to screen out inheritable genetic diseases. We document the genetic markers in a dog that uniquely identify our dogs and ensure our record keeping is correct. We test thyroids to make sure they are in a healthy range.

We do our best to try to breed the healthiest dogs possible. Things can still happen, we're dealing with genetics, but we've been very fortunate so far and I'm very careful in the breeding stock I select. And I carefully select which dogs I mate to each other. Because of these tests I will hopefully never produce a puppy that is affected with PRA, for example.

Again, our goal with every breeding we do is to create a better dog. With every breeding we do we want to protect, preserve and enhance the wonderful qualities that make up an Australian Labradoodle.

The Labradoodle Associations have set guidelines for breeding healthy dogs as well. I belong to the two major organizations – the Australian Labradoodle Association of America (ALAA) and the Australian Labradoodle Club of America (ALCA). The ALAA has developed a "Paw System" based on the level of health testing a breeder does. I'm proud to say we test to the highest level and have achieved both the gold and silver paws every year since we founded California Labradoodles and the paw system was implemented.

Is it possible to describe a fairly typical Labradoodle so people know what to expect?

Our Australian Labradoodles are consistently sweet, loving, oh so intelligent and eager to please. They are devoted to their people, and happy sitting by your side or accompanying you on a walk. They are easy to train as they want to make you happy. They love people and have a somewhat comical, goofy and joyful personality. They are happy dogs.

Australian Labradoodles range from mellow to active, they tend to be enthusiastic when people play with them, and their families walk into a room, and mellow the rest of the time. When we select our breeding stock, calmness is something I really look for. We are breeding for calmness and we like to hold pups that we think would make good therapy dogs. I want the calm, sweet, loving, confident puppy that will let me do anything to him, place him on his back, put my hands in his mouth, etc, when I'm selecting my breeding stock.

Can you offer advice to people looking to buy a Labradoodle, and how much do they cost?

Make sure you buy from a responsible breeder who invests their time and money into caring for their pups. That means they do extensive health testing on the parents, expose their pups to as many sights and sounds of the world as possible, and raise the pups in their home, not in a kennel situation. I'd advise people to look for breeders who belong to either the ALAA or the ALCA and breed to the highest standards, following the ethics of both organizations. Look for people who do the maximum, not the minimum, health testing.

Make sure the dog lives in the breeder's home, that your puppy doesn't come from a kennel. We use guardian families to help us raise our pups. We place our care dogs into their guardian homes between 8 and 12 weeks of age, with the goal of placing them right away into their forever homes. By using guardian families, I ensure that each pup in my breeding program gets a loving, caring home to grow up in. Typically a female will have three litters prior to retirement, sometimes four. We usually retire our dogs around ages 5 or 6.

We are looking for families who will keep us well informed of how the puppy is growing up, who will take excellent care of our puppy and ensure they are well-loved and well-trained.

We use the words care family and guardian family interchangeably to describe our program. We are not a kennel, nor do we ever want to become one. We only have three female dogs that live with us in our home – Rosie, Nectar and Zena. Rosie and Nectar are spayed and retired and are our personal pets. Zena is our only breeding dog here. All the rest of our dogs live in carefully selected care homes. That way each and every dog in our breeding program, is a loved and important member of their own family and gets all the individual attention and pampering they need. And that ensures that we also have lots of love and attention to go around whenever our care family girls or boys come for a visit.

You asked about pricing. We haven't raised our prices in 8 years. My prices are right in line with other quality Australian Labradoodle breeders. I spend a lot of money health testing my dogs, training my dogs, socializing my dogs and caring for my dogs, and I imported all my original breeding stock from Australia.

Breeding is expensive if done right. We don't cut corners on anything. Australian Labradoodles typically live between 14 and 16 years, so it is helpful for some people to amortize the cost over time. The majority of the money we make goes right back into the dogs. People can expect to pay upwards of $2500 or more for an Australian Labradoodle. There are breeders who charge more than I do, and breeders who charge less. I believe my prices are lower than they should be. Just ask good questions of whatever breeder you go with, and make sure the breeder knows what is behind their lines, that the dogs are from quality breeding stock, and that the breeder has done extensive health testing on their dogs, as well as spent time and money on the puppies care and socialization.

What colors and sizes are most popular?

I think my clients are pretty evenly split between wanting miniatures or medium sized pups. We breed both. Our most popular colors are reds, apricots, caramels and chocolates, but all colors are beautiful. For example, we price our blacks and creams a bit less because they don't photograph as well, and we have less demand for them, but everyone falls in love with them when they meet them in person and see how beautiful they are.

As a breed expert, are there any 'essential' tips you would like to share with new owners?

When training puppies it's all about love, consistency and timing. The day you bring your puppy home, is a good time to call a dog trainer and schedule her first obedience class. Australian Labradoodles are extremely intelligent and time spent training her now will really pay off.

Puppies need to know their place in the pack, and need to be at the bottom of the pack. Your family is her pack now and even the smallest child needs to be above her in the pack. Get your children involved in her training. It's important they work with the dog trainer too. Reward the good behavior and ignore the mistakes. Praise her when she does something right! Routines are really important for pups so they learn what is expected of them. The closer you stick to a schedule initially, the better she'll be. You'll want to get her into your schedule, and at the beginning consistency will be important for her success.

You don't want to give a puppy the run of the house, until she knows where to potty. If a puppy has an accident in your house and you find it, you can't show it to them and expect them to understand. They have no idea who did that and what you are upset about. Even one second later is too late. You have to catch the puppy in the act. As they have the accident, tell them no gently but firmly, and then carry them to where you want them to potty and praise her profusely. Please don't scold her if she has an accident in the house or does something you don't like. It's not her fault. She doesn't know where to go at your house yet, and she doesn't know the rules. Give her time.

Our pups are smart. Be careful or they will train you. If you come to a puppy when they whine, they learn quickly that whining brings you running to them. Again reward the good behavior, ignore the bad.

Pups can have a vocabulary like a two year old. Use words to mark their actions – good sit, good down, good come, good leave it, good quiet, good off, good spin, good high five. Whatever you want them to learn, give it a word.

Teach children to sit on their bottoms when they hold her. Teach them to always approach her from the front so she sees them coming. Teach kids to pet her gently.

Again, with puppies, it's all about consistency and timing. With a puppy, it's important you get the timing right. If you teach a dog to sit and say good sit as she's getting up to get her treat, she learns sit means get the treat. You have to reward her whether by words or treats the second her bottom hits the ground.

When you bring your puppy home, take her everywhere with you. The more sights and sounds she experiences, and the more people and dogs that she meets, the better socialized and better mannered dog she will become. The first year of life is critical to their development. They need to see and explore the world from the first day they come into your home. They are little sponges as young puppies, and the more you introduce her to, and teach her when she comes to your home, the better canine citizen she will be.

Thanks so much Dana for sharing your expertise and for sharing your unique story with everyone.

Dana Eckert of California Labradoodles
http://www.californialabradoodles.us/

Bonus Chapter 2 - Interview With Nicki Dana

How long have you been breeding and where are you based?

I am based in lovely sunny Central California, roughly half way between Los Angeles and the San Francisco Bay Area. We have a home in the country and enjoy taking our dogs on hikes in the hills and to the nearby beaches.

I spent several years working as an Animal Control Officer for the county which included among other things, duties of picking up stray animals, advising owners on how to work with their animals, cruelty cases and kennel inspections. The kennels I inspected ranged from pet stores, to professional kennels, to home-based breeders to "back-yard breeders." I saw the good, bad and the ugly. The good breeders were doing it right and standing by their dogs and programs. I knew I wanted to breed in the future and join the ranks of the good breeders. I just needed to find the right breed for me.

Once I learned of the Labradoodle, I began researching the breed. I thought a Labradoodle might be a good fit for my family, country lifestyle and my breeding plans. Nine years ago I purchased my first F1 (first generation) Labradoodle with breeding rights, and if she grew into what I thought she would be and her health testing was good, I would get started. She is/was wonderful and when she was old enough I began my breeding career with her.

Do you specialise in one type of Labradoodle or several different types?

I breed the Australian Labradoodle now, however I continue to include healthy infusions of early generation dogs to move away from some of the highly used Australian lines from a few of the large founding kennels.

Why does the Labradoodle breed seem to have so much division between breeders of different types of Labradoodle?

There is always some division between a group of people even when relatively working together. These differences can range from our specific breeding plans, how we house and socialize our dogs and puppies, which health testing we use or consider important, customer service, etc. It does not mean one breeder is right and another wrong, it's just different. This goes for our dogs as well. While I may not think a stud is nice enough to use, he may have important genes for another person's breeding program. Many people adore F1 or F1b Labradoodles. Other breeders like Australian Labradoodles with infusions of more than 3 foundation breeds. Some breeders have decided to add other foundation breeds in the mix and call the Labradoodle by another name. These aren't right or wrong, just different breeding programs.

The key difference is between the American Labradoodle (F1) and the Australian Labradoodle – I think many readers will not be aware of the differences, in your opinion how do they differ in practical terms?

American Labradoodle isn't really a term that most breeders are using. It's either Labradoodle or Australian Labradoodle and there are early generation dogs and multi-generational dogs of both.

An F1 Labradoodle is a first generation cross between a Labrador and a Poodle. These early generational crosses are wonderful in their own right, but tend to be not consistent in coat. You may get a flat shedding coat like a Lab, or a silky shedding coat, or a short wispy coat that is low shedding. These coats are very easy to care for and only require a quick brushing daily and don't mat, so there is a plus side. An F1 also would tend to be more similar to a Labrador in size.

An F1 may be bred with a Poodle to create an F1b which would normally have a non-shedding, wool or fleece curly coat. Breeders may do this to solidify a non-shed coat and allergy friendliness which Poodles are known for. I have found it easiest to keep the dogs with curly coats kept relatively short for ease of care.

An F1 may also be bred to another F1 or multi-generational Labradoodle or Australian Labradoodle. These pairings normally have lovely offspring and can add new genes to a breeder's program.

The multi-generational Labradoodle and Australian Labradoodle have a much more consistent look both in coat and structure. Normally the Australian Labradoodlle will have a more stocky build than the Labradoodle. Both should have great non-shed coats and lovely dispositions. Although there are variances in different breeding programs these dogs will be easily recognizable as multi-generational Labradoodles or Australian Labradoodles.

Do you think the breed is becoming more popular or less as time goes on – perhaps offer your thoughts on how you see the breed progressing?

I have not noticed any fluctuation of popularity yet. I think the breed is still experiencing the popularity of being the last "new thing" and many people want to keep up with what the neighbors have. Add that to the Labradoodle's adorable looks from puppy to adult and generally sweet personality and you have a very popular dog breed. Having said that, the Labradoodle and Australian Labradoodle is not a good match for everyone who wants one.

Why would new owners choose a Labradoodle over say, a more mainstream (AKC) breed?

I think Labradoodles are mainstream now. Many people are drawn to the idea of an adorable, well-rounded dog with a non-shedding coat. I also find some people with allergies aren't affected as much with a Labradoodle, although each person should spend time with a specific dog to see how it affects them. There is no reason that these people couldn't find another breed to enjoy as other breeds have some of the same characteristics, but as a whole the Labradoodle has the entire package.

Are new owners concerned at all that the Labradoodle is not recognized by the American Kennel Club?

I have not had more than a few new or prospective owners even ask about the breed being recognized by AKC. Both Labradoodle and Australian Labradoodle are recognized by the Continental Kennel Club (CKC) of which I am a Preferred Breeder Member for registration purposes. They are also recognized by the Orthopedic Foundation for Animals (OFA). There are also breed clubs such as the Australian Labradoodle Association of America (ALAA), which I belong to, and the Australian Labradoodle Club of America (ALCA). Both clubs have high standards for dog care, health testing requirements and Breeder Code of Ethics regarding the way animals and customers are treated.

What type of health issues can a Labradoodle have and how do you deal with preventing these?

Just like any dog breed, a Labradoodle or Australian Labradoodle would be susceptible to the same conditions that afflict the foundation breeds. These are primarily hip, elbow and eye issues, however as new issues arise in the foundation breeds, they also arise in the Labradoodle. Breeders can have a multitude of tests done on their breeding dogs to try minimize the risk of creating afflicted offspring. I have my breeding dogs' hips and elbows evaluated along with patella, thyroid and cardiac function. Their eyes are examined by a veterinary ophthalmologist. I also have various genetic testing done to aid in my breeding decisions.

Is it possible to describe a fairly typical Labradoodle so people know what to expect?

There really isn't a "typical Labradoodle" because there are so many variables in genetics, socializing, exercise opportunities and training.

Overall, I would say they are very smart, sweet and want to be with their people. They do require a daily purposeful walk for exercise to drain energy if living in a smaller home. They tend to be easy to train. This means they learn everything quickly. I had an owner proudly report how their puppy learned to ring the poochie bells to go outside for potty after one day. Recently that same owner reported how he caught his now larger puppy trying to turn the doorknob!

I try to breed for a calmer personality but also for athleticism. I like a dog that is settled indoors but yet willing to go for a long run or hike with me. I should mention that most Labradoodles are extremely fast runners.

Grooming can also vary and be a matter of personal taste. I have found that country dogs tend to be kept in shorter coat with a periodic shave down than city dogs with a longer coat who get a regular scissor clip at the groomers. The shedding dogs need brushing more often but it is easier to do. The non-shedding dogs need brushing to prevent matting.

People should try to pick their new family member by an honest evaluation of who, when and how they will be caring for their dog and what they hope to do with their dog. Some people are looking for a therapy dog and others an agility dog and others just a great gentle family companion. They must share their intentions with the breeder who can say whether or not their dogs would be a good fit. I would be leery of a breeder that says all of their dogs would be good with every family. I do allow families to select their puppy out of a litter, however I also reserve the right to veto a bad choice. It is so important to get a good fit for the family.

How much do your puppies cost?

The average price for a quality Australian Labradoodle from a reputable breeder tends to run about $2,500. I have seen people charging a little less or a little more, depending on what they have or the health testing or guarantee they offer. The earlier generation dogs or those with inconsistent coats tend to be priced lower. Most of that goes back into maintaining our quality breeding program.

What colors and sizes are most sought after?

Color and size requests seems to go in phases and is really just a personal preference. Families living in urban areas tend to prefer the mini and medium size dogs. Families in more rural settings like the medium to standard sizes. The shades of chocolate are consistently pretty popular. Some people find the black, blue or silver just adorable. Many like the cream, apricot and red. Just the other day I had a request for all white. I have found that often people think they would like a certain color based on photos but when they see the dogs or puppies face to face, they are just as likely to select a different option.

As a breed expert, are there any 'essential' tips you would like to share with new owners?

I send all pups home with instructions to start training right away, set firm consistent boundaries and to regularly drain energy. Just like with children, a bored mind, not enough boundaries and too much energy are recipes for a quick disaster.

Are there things that you see owners doing that frustrate you?

Most people seeking Labradoodles have the absolute best intentions and love their furry family members and really want to do the best thing for them. I think the thing that I find the most common that I need to help with is the new owner that treats their pup like a much older dog with too many freedoms and choices. Puppies and young dogs need to know their boundaries and that the human is in charge. If the human isn't calmly and firmly making that clear a young dog will try to step up to take the role. Like a teenager, part of that happens as the dog matures but how they come through that phase is up to the family.

Do you have any advice on bringing home a puppy, training and settling him into your home?

The first few days should be pretty calm and with immediate family only. Pup should have plenty of rest time. I advise people to settle the pup into a small space so it's not overwhelmed. Preferably it should be where the family spends a lot of time such as a kitchen or family room. There is plenty of time later to introduce pup to friends and extended family and expose pup to the rest of the house.

What would be the positives and negatives of owning a Labradoodle would you say?

There are so many positives. These dogs are so beautiful, smart, athletic, gentle and loving. Their coats are so soft and feel so great you could love on them for hours. I love the non-shedding. I love having dogs that want to do whatever I am feeling like doing at the time. They are just so willing and as long as they have initial training and mental stimulation, some exercise and occasional grooming (depending on coat type and length), they are just perfect.

The warning I give all our Labradoodle families is that they need to get used to stopping and talking to strangers. Everyone will want to ask about the Labradoodle and pet them.

What feeding routines and types of food/supplements do you recommend?

I don't recommend a particular type of food and/or supplement. We feed a good quality puppy chow and provide resources for people to find a food that works well for their own situation. We recommend that people feed their pups 4 times a day initially. Adults should eat twice a day.

Nicki, thank you for taking the time to share your tips and knowledge of the Labradoodle.

Nicki Dana of Premiere Labradoodles
http://premierelabradoodles.com

Relevant Websites

Australian Labradoodle Association
http://www.laa.org.au

Australian Labradoodle Association of America (ALAA)
http://alaa-labradoodles.com

Australian Labradoodle Club of America (ALCA)
http://www.australianlabradoodleclub.us

The Labradoodle Club of Great Britain (LCGB)
http://www.labradoodleclubofgreatbritain.co.uk

The UK Australian Labradoodle Club (UKALC)
http://www.ukaustralianlabradoodleclub.co.uk

UK Doodle Club
http://www.uk-doodleclub.com

The UK Labradoodle Association
http://www.labradoodle.org.uk

Photo Credit: Amy Schuning of AKA's Doodles & Poodles

Glossary

Abdomen – The surface area of a dog's body lying between the chest and the hindquarters; also referred to as the belly.

Allergy – An abnormally sensitive reaction to substances including pollens, foods or microorganisms. May be present in humans or animals with similar symptoms including, but not limited to, sneezing, itching and skin rashes.

Anal Glands – Glands located on either side of a dog's anus used to mark territory. May become blocked and require treatment by a veterinarian.

Arm – On a dog, the region between the shoulder and the elbow is referred to as the arm or the upper arm.

Artificial Insemination – The process by which semen is artificially introduced into the reproductive tract of a female dog for the purposes of a planned pregnancy.

Back – That portion of a dog's body that extends from the withers (or shoulder) to the croup (approximately the area where the back flows into the tail.)

Backyard Breeder – Any person engaged in the casual breeding of purebred dogs with no regard to genetic quality or consideration of the breed standard is referred to as a backyard breeder.

Bat Ear – A dog's ear that stands upright from a broad base with a rounded top and a forward-facing opening.

Bitch – The appropriate term for a female dog.

Blooded – An accepted reference to a pedigreed dog.

Breed – A line or race of dogs selected and cultivated by man from a common gene pool to achieve and maintain a characteristic appearance and function.

Breed Standard – A written "picture" of a perfect specimen of a given breed in terms of appearance, movement and behavior as formulated by a parent organization, for example, the American Kennel Club or in Great Britain, The Kennel Club.

Brindle – A marking pattern typically described in conjunction with another color to achieve a layering of black hairs with a lighter color (fawn, brown, or gray) to produce a tiger-striped pattern.

Brows – The contours of the frontal bone that form ridges above a dog's eyes.

Buttocks – The hips or rump of a dog.

Castrate – The process of removing a male dog's testicles.

Chest – That portion of a dog's trunk or body encased by the ribs.

Coat – The hair covering a dog. Most breeds have both an outer coat and an undercoat.

Come into Season – The point at which a female dog becomes fertile for purposes of mating.

Congenital – Any quality, particularly an abnormality, present at birth.

Crate – Any portable container used to house a dog for transport or provided to a dog in the home as a "den."

Crossbred – Dogs are said to be crossbred when each of their parents is of a different breed.

Dam – A term for the female parent.

Dew Claw – The dew claw is an extra claw on the inside of the leg. It is a rudimentary fifth toe.

Euthanize – The act of relieving the suffering of a terminally ill animal by inducing a humane death, typically with an overdose of anesthesia.

Fancier – Any person with an exceptional interest in purebred dogs and the shows where they are exhibited.

Free Feeding – The practice of making a constant supply of food available for a dog's consumption. Not recommended with Labradoodles.

Groom – To make a dog's coat neat by brushing, combing or trimming.

Harness - A cloth or leather strap shaped to fit the shoulders and chest of a dog with a ring at the top for attaching a lead. An alternative to using a collar.

Haunch Bones – Terminology for the hip bones of a dog.

Haw – The membrane inside the corner of a dog's eye known as the third eyelid.

Head – The cranium and muzzle of a dog.

Hip Dysplasia – A condition in dogs due to a malformation of the hip resulting in painful and limited movement of varying degrees.

Hindquarters – The back portion of a dog's body, including the pelvis, thighs, hocks and paws.

Hock – Bones on the hind leg of a dog that form the joint between the second thigh and the metatarsus. Known as the dog's true heel.

Inbreeding – When two dogs of the same breed that are closely related mate.

Kennel – A facility where dogs are housed for breeding or an enclosure where dogs are kept.

Lead – Any strap, cord or chain used to restrain or lead a dog. Typically attached to a collar or harness. Also called a leash.

Litter – The puppy or puppies from a single birth or "whelping."

Muzzle – That portion of a dog's head lying in front of the eyes and consisting of the nasal bone, nostrils and jaws.

Neuter – To castrate or spay a dog, thus rendering them incapable of reproducing.

Pedigree – The written record of a pedigreed dog's genealogy. Should extend to three or more generations.

Puppy – Any dog of less than 12 months of age.

Puppy Mill – An establishment that exists for the purpose of breeding as many puppies for sale as possible with no consideration of potential genetic defects.

Rose Ear – Small ears that fold over and back revealing the burr.

Separation Anxiety – The anxiety and stress suffered by a dog left alone for any period of time.

Sire – The accepted term for the male parent.

Spay – The surgery to remove a female dog's ovaries to prevent conception.

Whelping – Term for the act of giving birth to puppies.

Withers – The highest point of a dog's shoulders.

Wrinkle – Any folding and loose skin on the forehead and foreface of a dog.

Photo Credit: Jeanette & Mike Parker of Chesapeake Miniature Labradoodles

Index

CPSIA information can be obtained
at www.ICGtesting.com
Printed in the USA
BVOW10s2348170817
492248BV00008B/211/P